Classic Stories
Love

Level 5

Retold by Chris Rice
Series Editors: Andy Hopkins and Jocelyn Potter

Pearson Education Limited
Edinburgh Gate, Harlow,
Essex CM20 2JE, England
and Associated Companies throughout the world.

ISBN 0 582 46578 8

This edition first published 2001

Typeset by Pantek Arts Ltd, Maidstone, Kent
Set in 11/14pt Bembo
Printed in Spain by Mateu Cromo, S.A. Pinto (Madrid)

Published by Pearson Education Limited in association with
Penguin Books Ltd, both companies being subsidiaries of Pearson Plc

Contents

Introduction

I am glad it cannot happen twice, the fever of love. It is a fever, and a misery too, whatever the poets may say. One is so easily hurt.

These are the words of Maxim de Winter's future wife in Daphne du Maurier's *Rebecca*, one of the great love stories of twentieth century literature. In this collection of extracts from books in the Penguin Readers series, you will read about some of the most famous love stories of all time: the relationships of Elizabeth Bennet and Mr Darcy, Heathcliff and Cathy, Jane Eyre and Mr Rochester, Othello and Desdemona, Romeo and Juliet, Dr Zhivago and Lara.

These stories show the many sides of love, and the many different reactions to it. Some people run away from it, others welcome it, and others pretend that it is not happening. But there is one feature that all these stories share: the power of love to shape our lives, whatever other plans we have made. It sometimes leads to tragedy; it sometimes leads to joy. The journey of life is never easy when love interrupts our plans; but without love, is the journey worth making at all?

Although the basic features of love stories have remained the same since the days of Shakespeare, different writers' treatment of the subject shows changing attitudes over the years. Before Shakespeare, in the fifteenth century, rich people married for financial or political reasons. Marriage was a business arrangement, and love was not a necessary part of it.

However, as new ideas about joining the mind and body in love and marriage developed, the status of women began to change. Shakespeare described the two different sides of this change. *The Taming of the Shrew* shows the traditional side of marriage as a business arrangement, while *Romeo and Juliet* shows the developing importance of romantic love in a relationship.

At the beginning of the nineteenth century, there were signs that people were beginning to put a higher value on love. They allowed themselves to follow their feelings more freely, and were less afraid of what society thought about their 'unsuitable' marriages. This made the older people, who still had a traditional attitude towards marriage, extremely angry. See how angry Lady Catherine de Bourgh (*Pride and Prejudice*) becomes when she thinks that her nephew is in danger of marrying for love, not money!

Love became increasingly important in marriage. Women were less happy to marry just for status and money. The most important thing in life for them was to find true love. If a woman wanted to win the love of the right man, she had to let the man be strong and in control. The tragedy of *Wuthering Heights*, for example, comes from the fact that Cathy loves a man who has a lower social status than she does. She cannot, therefore, be weak, and he cannot be in control. Their love has no chance of surviving, but it still refuses to die.

In the middle of the nineteenth century, with the development of capitalist economics, the new middle class began to grow rapidly and women began to gain economic freedoms that they had never had before. They began to have jobs and to be more independent. As a result, men had to pay more attention to what women wanted. In *The Warden*, for example, Eleanor Harding persuades the man who loves her, John Bold, to change his mind on a very important public matter. This would not have happened if she had lived in the days of Jane Austen.

However, as women's confidence and freedom grew, men often became increasingly doubtful and less confident. It was not enough for a man to be strong, rich and handsome. If he wanted success in love, he had to be more sensitive to a woman's needs.

This frightened some men away from love completely, and they found happiness in adventure instead (*The Prisoner of Zenda*, *Round the World in Eighty Days*). Other men struggled to understand women more, and became very confused and uncertain (Jude Fawley in *Jude the Obscure*, Paul Morell in *Sons and Lovers*).

In the twentieth century, a new age of romantic love grew. Romantic attraction became not only desirable but the only acceptable way of choosing a partner for life. Romantic love was the most difficult and complicated human relationship that had ever been attempted; it combined the tenderness of love with household cares and the raising of children. Novels showing how romantic love could survive in extremely difficult situations became increasingly popular. For example, in *Dr Zhivago*, the love between Yury and Lara survives war, revolution, separation and their love for their families. In *Rebecca*, the new Mrs de Winter's love for her husband is stronger than her fear and jealousy of his first wife.

Today, modern romantic love still remains almost everybody's goal. It is necessary for the satisfaction of our main emotional needs and happiness.

The extracts in this book, by some of the world's greatest writers, will show you many different sides of love in many different ages. You will read about the suffering and sadness, the jealousy and pain, the tragedy and loss that love can bring. But you will also read about its victories, its passion and excitement, its humour and its moments of great joy. In the end, however, it is probably the beauty of love that most of us remember.

And when you have read these extracts, why not try the full stories, all in the Penguin Readers series?

1 *Rebecca* Daphne du Maurier

Daphne du Maurier (1907–89) was born in London, but for most of her adult life she lived in the south-west of England. The wild weather and scenery of Cornwall provide the background and atmosphere for her tense, romantic mysteries. The most famous of her books are *Jamaica Inn* (1936), *Rebecca* (1938) and *My Cousin Rachel* (1951). In 1963 Alfred Hitchcock made a classic film of her short story *The Birds*.

Rebecca is basically the story of a woman's desire to please her husband. Strangely, the young woman who narrates the story is never given a name. At the time of this short extract, she is in Monte Carlo as the paid companion of an older woman. She describes her feelings when she meets and falls in love with Maxim de Winter, a wealthy man whose wife, Rebecca, has recently died.

First love

I was happy that afternoon; I can remember it well. I can see the blue sky and sea. I can feel again the wind on my face, and hear my laugh, and his that answered it. It was not the Monte Carlo that I had known before. The harbour was a dancing thing, bright with boats, and the sailors were cheerful, smiling men, careless as the wind. I can clearly remember my comfortable, badly fitting suit, my broad hat, the shoes I wore. I had never looked more youthful; I had never felt so old. . . .

. . . I am glad it cannot happen twice, the fever of first love. It is a fever, and a misery too, whatever the poets may say. One is so easily hurt.

I have forgotten much of Monte Carlo, of those morning drives, of where we went, even of our conversation; but I have not

1

forgotten how my fingers shook, pulling on my hat, and how I ran down the stairs and so outside. He was always there, in the driver's seat, reading a paper while he waited, and when he saw me he always smiled, and threw the paper behind him into the back seat. Then he opened the door, saying, 'Well, how is the companion this morning, and where does she want to go?' If he had driven round in circles it would not have mattered to me.

◆

The young girl marries Maxim de Winter and returns with him to Manderley, his lovely country home. But then her problems begin. She feels threatened by the constant presence of Rebecca's memory in the house, and begins to doubt her husband's love for her. She also cannot understand why Mrs Danvers, the house-keeper, dislikes her so much.

In this extract, the new Mrs de Winter hopes to please her husband, Maxim, at their fancy dress dance.

The fancy dress dance

The preparations went on for the dance. Maxim and Frank were busy every morning and I began to worry about what I was going to wear. It seemed so silly not to be able to think of anything. One evening, when I was changing for dinner, there was a knock at my bedroom door. I called 'Come in,' thinking it was my servant, Clarice. It was Mrs Danvers.

'I hope you will forgive me for interrupting you,' she said. 'Have you decided yet, madam, what you will wear?'

There was a suggestion of scorn in her voice, of strange satisfaction. She had probably heard from Clarice that I still had no ideas.

'No. I haven't decided.'

'Why don't you copy the clothes from one of the pictures in the hall?'

'Yes. I might think about that.' I wondered why such an idea had not come to me before. It was an obvious solution to my problem.

'All the pictures in the hall would be easy to copy, especially that one of the young lady in white, with her hat in her hand.' Her voice was surprisingly normal. Did she want to be friends with me at last? Or did she realize that it was not I who had told Maxim about Favell, and was this her way of thanking me for my silence? 'Has Mr de Winter not suggested anything for you?'

'No. No, I want to surprise him and Mr Crawley.'

'When you do decide, I advise you to have your dress made in London. Voce, in Bond Street, is a good place I know. I should study the pictures in the hall, madam, especially the one I mentioned. And you needn't think that I'll tell anyone. Your secret will be safe with me.'

'Thank you, Mrs Danvers.' I went on dressing, confused by her manner, and wondering if I had the unpleasant Favell to thank for it.

When I looked at the picture, I saw that the clothes in it were lovely, and would be easy to copy. It was a painting by Raeburn of Caroline de Winter, who had been a famous London beauty in the eighteenth century. She wore a simple white dress. The hat might be rather difficult, but I could carry it in my hand, as she did. I would have to wear a hairpiece. My hair would never curl in that way. Perhaps Voce in London would do the whole thing. It was a relief to decide at last. . . .

. . . Clarice could hardly control her excitement, and I began to feel the same as the great day came near. Beatrice and her husband were coming to stay the night, and a lot of other people were coming to dinner before the dance began.

I found Clarice waiting for me in my room, her round face red with excitement. We laughed at each other like schoolgirls. The dress fitted perfectly.

'It's lovely, madam – fit for the Queen of England!'

'Give me the curls carefully. Don't spoil them.' With shaking fingers I made the finishing touches. 'Oh, Clarice, what will Mr de Winter say?' I did not recognize the face that I saw in the mirror. The eyes were larger, surely, the mouth thinner, the skin white and clear? The curls stood away from the head in a little cloud. I watched this person that was not me at all, and then smiled; a new, slow smile.

'They've gone down,' said Clarice. 'They're all standing in the hall. Mr de Winter, Captain and Mrs Lacy, and Mr Crawley.' I went along the passage and looked down, hidden from view at the top of the stairs.

'I don't know what she's doing,' Maxim was saying, 'she's been up in the bedroom for hours.'

The band were near me, getting their instruments ready.

'Tell the drummer to play his drum,' I whispered, 'and then shout out "Miss Caroline de Winter".' What fun it was! Suddenly the sound of the drum filled the great hall; I saw them look up, surprised.

'Miss Caroline de Winter!' shouted the drummer.

I came forward to the top of the stairs and stood there, smiling, my hat in my hand like the girl in the picture. I waited for the laughter and shouts of approval that would follow as I walked slowly down the stairs. Nobody moved. They all stared at me, speechless. Beatrice gave a little cry and put her hand to her mouth. I went on smiling.

'How do you do, Mr de Winter?' I said.

Maxim had not moved. He looked up at me, his glass in his hand. All the colour left his face. I stopped, one foot on the next stair. Something was wrong. They had not understood. Why was Maxim looking like that? Why did they all stand as still as stone?

Then Maxim moved forward, his eyes never leaving my face. 'What the devil do you think you are doing?' His eyes flashed with anger. His face was grey. I could not move.

'It's the picture,' I said. 'It's the picture – the one in the hall.'

There was a long silence. We went on looking at each other. Nobody moved in the hall. I swallowed; my hand moved to my throat. 'What is it?' I said. 'What have I done?'

Why were they looking at me like that with dull, expressionless faces? Why didn't anybody say something? When Maxim spoke again, I did not recognize his voice. It was quiet, cold as ice – not a voice I knew.

'Go and change,' he said. 'It doesn't matter what you put on. Find an ordinary evening dress – anything will do. Go now, before anybody else comes.'

I could not speak. I went on looking at him. His eyes were the only living things in his dead, grey face.

'What are you standing there for?' His voice was ugly and strange. 'Didn't you hear what I said?'

I turned and ran blindly down the passage behind me. Clarice had gone. Tears filled my eyes. Then I saw Mrs Danvers. I shall never forget the expression on her face – the face of a victorious devil. She stood there, smiling at me. And then I ran from her, down the long passage to my own room.

2 *A Midsummer Night's Dream*
from *Tales from Shakespeare*
Charles and Mary Lamb

William Shakespeare (1564–1616) was born in Stratford-upon-Avon, and by 1592 he was famous in London as an actor and writer. Over the next twenty years he wrote thirty-eight plays; most of these are considered to be masterpieces. He also wrote a lot of great poetry. Four hundred years later, he is still the most popular and famous writer in the English language.

In 1807 Charles Lamb and his sister, Mary Lamb, were asked to write the stories from the best known of Shakespeare's plays in a way that children could easily understand. Their adaptations of the stories were a great success.

A Midsummer Night's Dream (1596) is the most popular of all Shakespeare's comedies. Egeus wants his daughter, Hermia, to marry Demetrius, but Hermia is in love with Lysander. When the King of Athens threatens her with death if she refuses to obey her father, Hermia decides to run away with Lysander. She tells her friend, Helena, of her plans. Helena, who loves Demetrius, tells him, and the four young people run away into a wood outside Athens. In the wood Oberon, King of the Fairies, hears Helena begging Demetrius to love her. He feels sorry for Helena, and tells Puck, his helper, to put love-juice into Demetrius's eyes so that he will love Helena when he wakes up.

Lysander falls in love with the wrong woman

Hermia escaped from her father's house that night, to avoid the death that she faced for refusing to marry Demetrius. When she entered the wood, she found her dear Lysander waiting for her to take her to his aunt's house. But before they were halfway through the wood, Hermia was so tired that Lysander made her rest until morning on the soft green grass. And, lying down himself on the ground a little distance away, they soon fell fast asleep.

Here they were soon found by Puck. Puck saw a good-looking young man asleep. Noticing that his clothes were made in the Athenian way and that a pretty lady was sleeping near him, he thought that this must be the Athenian girl and her cruel lover, whom Oberon had sent him to find. He therefore supposed that, as they were alone together, she would be the first thing he would see when he awoke; so, without delay, he poured some of the juice of the little purple flower into his eyes. But it happened that Helena came that way and, instead of Hermia, she was the first thing Lysander saw when he opened his eyes. And, strangely, so powerful was the love-spell that all his love for Hermia disappeared, and Lysander fell in love with Helena.

If he had seen Hermia first when he awoke, the mistake Puck made would not have mattered, as he could not love that lady too well. But for poor Lysander to be forced by a fairy love-spell to forget his own true Hermia, and to run after another lady and leave Hermia asleep alone in a wood at midnight, was very sad. . . .

. . . The misfortune happened in this way. Helena tried to stay with Demetrius when he ran away from her so rudely, but she could not continue this unequal race for long, since men are always better runners in a long race than women. So Helena soon lost sight of Demetrius; and while she was wandering around in a sad and lonely way, she arrived at the place where Lysander was sleeping.

'Ah!' said she. 'This is Lysander lying on the ground. Is he dead or asleep?' Then, gently touching him, she said, 'Good sir, if you are alive, awake.'

Lysander opened his eyes and, as the love-juice began to work, immediately spoke to Helena words of the wildest love and admiration; he told her that her beauty was even greater than Hermia's, and that he would run through fire for her. Helena, knowing Lysander was her friend Hermia's lover, and that he had promised to marry her, was very angry when she heard herself spoken to in this manner; she thought (as one can imagine) that Lysander was making a fool of her.

'Oh!' she said angrily. 'Why was I born to be laughed at by everyone? Is it not enough, is it not enough, young man, that I can never get a sweet look or a kind word from Demetrius? Must you now, sir, must you pretend in this cruel manner to love me? I thought, Lysander, you were too kind for that.' She ran away and Lysander followed her, completely forgetting his own Hermia, who was still asleep.

3   *The Courtship of Susan Bell*   **Anthony Trollope**
from *Outstanding Short Stories*

Anthony Trollope (1815–82) had a successful career in the Post Office. (He designed the red post box, which is still familiar in English streets.) He is, of course, more famous as a writer. His descriptions of provincial middle class life were very popular with the reading public, and his best work shows a sensitive and detailed understanding of human nature.

Unlike most of Trollope's stories, *The Courtship of Susan Bell* takes place in America. Aaron Dunn, a young engineer, falls in love with Susan Bell, his landlady's daughter. Aaron is a quiet man, afraid of women. He is nervous about the constant presence of Susan's mother and her sister, Hetta. How can he show Susan that he loves her when he is too shy even to talk to her?

Aaron Dunn's gift for Susan Bell

It was at the end of the second month when Aaron took another step – a dangerous step. In the evenings he still went on with his drawing for an hour or two; but for three or four evenings he did not ask anyone to look at what he was doing. One Friday he sat over his work until late, without any reading or talking at all; so late that at last Mrs Bell said, 'If you're going to sit much longer, Mr Dunn . . .'

'I've finished now,' said Aaron; and he looked carefully at the paper on which he had put his colours. 'I've finished now.' He paused for a moment, but then he carried the paper up to his bedroom with the rest. It was clear that it was intended as a present for Susan Bell.

The question which Aaron asked himself that night was this: should he offer the drawing to Susan in the presence of her mother and sister, or on some other occasion when they might be alone together? They had never been alone together yet, but Aaron thought they might be.

But he did not want to make it seem important. His first intention had been to throw the drawing carelessly across the table when it was completed, and to treat it as nothing. But he had finished it with more care than he had at first intended, and then he had paused when he had finished it. It was too late now to be careless about it.

On the Saturday evening when he came down from his room, Mr Beckard was there, and there was no opportunity that night. On the Sunday he went to church and walked with the family. This pleased Mrs Bell; but Sunday was not a suitable day for the picture.

On Monday the matter had become important to him. Things always do when they are delayed. Before tea that evening, when he came down, only Mrs Bell and Susan were in the room. He knew Hetta was his enemy, and therefore he decided to take this opportunity.

'Miss Susan,' he said slowly, his face burning with embarrassment. 'I have done a little drawing which I want you to accept.'

'Oh! I'm not sure,' said Susan, who had seen the red face.

Mrs Bell had seen it too, and pressed her lips together and looked serious. If he had not paused, and if he had not gone red in the face, she would probably have thought it quite unimportant.

Aaron saw immediately that his little gift would not be accepted easily. But he picked it out of his other papers and brought it to Susan. He tried to hand it to her carelessly, but I cannot say that he succeeded.

It was a very pretty coloured drawing of the same bridge, but with more details. In Susan's eyes it was a work of high art. She had seen few pictures, and her liking for the artist no doubt added to her admiration. But the more she admired it and wished for it, the stronger was her feeling that she ought not to take it.

Poor Susan! She stood for a minute looking at the drawing, but she said nothing; not even a word of praise. She felt that she was red in the face, and impolite to their guest; but her mother was looking at her and she did not know how to behave.

Mrs Bell put out her hand for the drawing, trying to think how to refuse the present politely. She took a moment to look at it.

'Oh, dear, Mr Dunn, it is very pretty; quite a beautiful picture. I cannot let Susan take that from you. You must keep it for some of your own special friends.'

'But I did it for her,' said Aaron.

Susan looked down at the ground, half pleased with the words. The drawing would look pretty on her bedroom wall. But the matter was now in her mother's hands.

'I am afraid it is too valuable, sir, for Susan to accept.'

'It is not valuable at all,' said Aaron, refusing to take it back from the woman's hand.

'Oh, I am quite sure it is. It is worth ten dollars at least – or twenty,' said poor Mrs Bell. The picture now lay on the tablecloth.

'It is not worth ten cents,' said Aaron. 'But as we had been talking about the bridge, I thought Miss Susan would accept it.'

'Accept what?' said Hetta, who had just come in. And then her eyes fell on the drawing and she picked it up.

'It is beautifully done,' said Mrs Bell gently. 'I am telling Mr Dunn that we can't take a present of anything so valuable.'

'Oh, no,' said Hetta. 'It wouldn't be right.'

It was a cold evening in March, and the fire was burning brightly. Aaron Dunn took up the drawing quietly – very quietly – and, rolling it up, put it between the burning pieces of wood. It was the work of four evenings, and the best picture he had ever done.

Susan, when she saw what he had done, burst into tears. Her mother felt ready to do the same, but she was able to control herself and only cried, 'Oh, Mr Dunn!'

'Mr Dunn is allowed to burn his own picture if he wants to,' said Hetta.

Aaron immediately felt ashamed of what he had done; and he also would have cried if he had not been a man. He walked away to one of the windows and looked out at the night. The stars were bright, and he thought that he would like to be walking fast by himself along the railway towards Balston. There he stood, perhaps for three minutes. He thought it would be proper to give Susan time to stop her tears.

'Will you please come to your tea, sir?' said Mrs Bell.

He turned round to do so, and found that Susan was gone. She had not been able to stop her tears. And the drawing had been so beautiful! It had been done especially for her too! And there had been something – she did not know what – in his eyes as he had said so. She had watched him closely during those four evenings' work; it was something very special, she was sure, and she had learned that all the careful work had been for her. Now all that work was destroyed. How was it possible not to cry?

4 *Round the World in Eighty Days* Jules Verne

Jules Verne (1828–1905) is often considered to be the father of science fiction. His books were originally written in French, and they show his passion for exploring possible new ways of travelling. *Five Weeks in a Balloon* (1863) was his first big success, followed by *A Journey to the Centre of the Earth* (1864) and *Twenty Thousand Leagues Under the Sea* (1870).

Round the World in Eighty Days (1873) is probably his best-loved book. Phileas Fogg and his faithful servant, Passepartout, attempt to win a bet by travelling around the world in eighty days.

In this extract, Fogg has arrived back in London with Passepartout and Aouda, a Princess whom he saved from death in

India. Fogg has lost his bet, and is left with no money. But, always a gentleman, he reacts calmly and bravely to his failure.

Phileas Fogg and Princess Aouda

A room in the house in Savile Row was prepared for Aouda, who was extremely unhappy. From certain words that she had heard Mr Fogg say, she guessed that he was thinking of putting an end to his life. For this reason Passepartout watched his master closely.

The night passed. Mr Fogg had gone to bed, but had he slept? Aouda could not sleep at all. Passepartout had watched, like a loyal dog, at his master's door all night.

Next morning, Mr Fogg called him and told him to make Aouda's breakfast. He asked to be excused from seeing her, as he needed to put his business in order. He would not come down, but in the evening he would like to speak to Aouda for a few moments.

Passepartout looked at his master and was unable to leave the room. His heart was heavy. He blamed himself more than ever for this sad ending to the adventure. If he had warned his master about Fix's plans, Mr Fogg would certainly not have brought the detective with him to Liverpool, and then . . .

'Master! Mr Fogg!' he cried. 'Blame me. It is my fault that . . .'

'I blame nobody,' answered Phileas Fogg in the calmest of voices. 'Go.'

Passepartout went to Aouda and gave the message.

'My good friend, do not leave your master alone — not for a moment. You say that he wants to see me this evening?'

'Yes. I think that he wants to make arrangements for your protection in England.'

'Then we'll wait,' said she.

During the day the house seemed empty. Phileas Fogg did not

go to the club. Why should he go to the club? His old companions there were not expecting him. As he had not appeared at the club the evening before, at a quarter to nine, his bet was lost.

At half past seven in the evening, Mr Fogg asked whether Aouda would receive him, and a few moments later they were alone in the room.

For five minutes he said nothing. Then, raising his eyes, he said: 'Will you forgive me for bringing you to England? When I had the idea of bringing you away from the country that had become so dangerous for you, I was rich and expected to offer you a part of my fortune. Your life would have been happy and free. Now I am poor.'

'I know that, Mr Fogg,' answered the young lady, 'and I will ask you this: will you forgive me for following you, and – who knows – for being one of the causes of your failure?'

'It was impossible for you to stay in India, and for your safety it was necessary for you to get away.'

'Then, Mr Fogg,' she went on, 'it was not enough for you to save me from a terrible death – you thought it was your duty to take care of my future.'

'That is true, but I have been unfortunate. My plan now is to give you the little that I have left.'

'But you, Mr Fogg, what will you do?'

'I am in need of nothing for myself.'

'But do you know what you are going to do?'

'I shall do what is right for me to do.'

'A man such as you cannot ever be in real want. Your friends . . .'

'I have no friends.'

'Then I am sorry for you, Mr Fogg; it is sad to be without friends. It is said that misfortune can be borne when there are two to bear it.'

'They do say that.'

'Mr Fogg,' she then said, getting up and holding out her hand to him, 'will you have me as your friend? Will you have me as your wife?'

At these words Mr Fogg stood up. For a moment he shut his eyes. When he opened them again, he said simply: 'I love you. Yes, I love you and am yours!'

He called Passepartout, who came and saw his master and Aouda holding hands. The Frenchman understood, and his face filled with joy.

Mr Fogg asked him whether it was too late for him to call on the Reverend Samuel Wilson to make arrangements for a marriage.

Passepartout smiled. 'It is never too late,' he said. It was five minutes past eight. 'It will be for tomorrow, Monday,' he added.

'For tomorrow, Monday?' asked Mr Fogg, looking at Aouda.

'For tomorrow, Monday!' she answered.

Passepartout ran out of the house.

5   *Wuthering Heights*   **Emily Brontë**

Emily Brontë (1818–48) was the fifth of six children in a family of writers. After the death of two of her sisters, Maria and Elizabeth, Emily lived at home with her other sisters, Charlotte and Anne. The three girls educated themselves and saw little of other families. To make their quiet village life more interesting, the three girls began to invent stories. Emily's novel *Wuthering Heights* was published in 1847, the same year as Charlotte's *Jane Eyre* and Anne's *Agnes Grey*. Their brother, Branwell, died in September, 1848. At his funeral Emily caught a fever, and she died a couple of months later.

Wuthering Heights is a story of violent emotions, which shocked readers at the time. The fact that such violent emotions and actions were written by a woman makes this a strangely powerful story even today. At the beginning of the story,

Mr Earnshaw rescues Heathcliff from a life of poverty on the streets of Liverpool. He takes the boy home with him and treats him like his own children, Catherine and Hindley. When Mr Earnshaw dies, Hindley treats Heathcliff very badly. As he gets older, Heathcliff falls in love with Catherine, who returns his love. However, she feels she cannot marry him because he is rough and socially unacceptable. She decides instead to marry Edgar Linton, a rich neighbour.

In this extract, Cathy tells Nelly Dean (the servant who narrates the story) about the feelings that she has for Heathcliff.

Cathy's hopeless passion for Heathcliff

I was nursing Hareton (Cathy's nephew) on my knee, when Cathy put her head in at the door and whispered: 'Are you alone, Nelly?'

'Yes, miss.'

'Where's Heathcliff?'

'Doing his work outside.'

He did not call out that this was not true. Perhaps he was half asleep.

A long pause followed. A tear fell from Catherine's cheek.

'Oh!' she cried at last. 'I'm very unhappy!'

'That's a pity,' I replied. 'You're hard to please: so many friends and so few cares, and you can't make yourself happy.'

'Nelly, will you keep a secret?' She knelt down beside me. 'I want to know what I should do. Today Edgar Linton has asked me to marry him. I accepted him. Say whether I was wrong.'

'Do you love him?'

'Who can help it? Of course I do.'

'Why do you love him, Miss Cathy?'

'Well, because he's very good-looking, and pleasant to be with.'

'That's bad.'

'He'll be rich, and I shall like to be the greatest woman in the area.'

'Then why are you unhappy? Your brother will be pleased. The old lady and gentleman won't protest, I think. You will escape from a disorganized, comfortless home into a wealthy, respectable one. Where is the difficulty?'

'Here – and here!' replied Catherine, putting one hand on her forehead and the other on her breast. 'In whichever place the soul lives. In my soul and in my heart, I'm certain I'm wrong.'

She seated herself by me. Her face became sadder; her hands shook.

'I have no right to marry Edgar Linton, and if that wicked brother of mine had not brought Heathcliff to such a low state, I wouldn't have thought of it. It would degrade me to marry Heathcliff now, so he will never know I love him – not because he's good-looking, Nelly, but because he's more myself than I am.'

I heard a slight movement before the speech ended. I turned my head and saw Heathcliff rise from a seat and creep out. He had listened until he heard Catherine say it would degrade her to marry him.

I begged her to speak lower.

'Why?' she asked, looking around nervously.

'Joseph is here,' I answered, 'and I think that Heathcliff is about at this moment.'

'Oh, I hope he didn't hear me!' she said. 'Give me Hareton while you get the supper, and let me have it with you. I will feel much more comfortable if I can persuade myself that Heathcliff has no idea of my feelings. He hasn't, has he? He doesn't know what being in love is?'

'I see no reason why he shouldn't know as well as you,' I answered, 'and if you are his choice, he is the most unfortunate being that ever was born! As soon as you become Mrs Linton, he loses friend and love and all! Have you considered how you'll bear the separation, and how he'll bear to be left quite friendless in the world?'

'He – left friendless! We – separated! Not as long as I live! Edgar must get rid of his dislike of him. Nelly, have you ever considered the fact that if Heathcliff and I married, we would have nothing? But if I marry Edgar, I can help Heathcliff rise in life, and place him out of my brother's power.'

'With your husband's money? That's the worst reason you've given for being the wife of young Linton.'

'It's not! It's the best! This is for one who . . . I can't explain it; but surely you and everybody have an idea that there is or should be an existence of yours beyond you? My great miseries in this world have been Heathcliff's miseries: my life is his. If everything else were destroyed, and he remained, I should still continue to be; and if everything else remained and he were gone, the universe would seem a stranger. My love for Edgar is like the leaves in the wood: time will change it, as the winter changes the trees. My love for Heathcliff is like the unchanging rocks beneath: a cause of little conscious pleasure, but necessary to my being. Nelly, I am Heathcliff! He's always in my mind, as part of me.'

'If I can make any sense of your nonsense, miss, it only causes me to believe that either you know nothing of a wife's duties, or else you are a wicked girl.'

◆

Cathy marries Edgar Linton and is going to have a baby. Heathcliff, mad with jealousy, runs away with Edgar's sister, Isabella, and marries her. Cathy becomes very ill because of all the unhappiness around her. Finally, Heathcliff is unable to stay away from Cathy any longer. Nelly Dean continues the story.

Catherine sat in a loose white dress, at the open window as usual. Her long hair, cut shorter during her illness, was simply combed over her forehead and neck. Her appearance was changed, but when she was calm there seemed a strange beauty in the change. The flash in her eyes had given place to a dreamy softness. The paleness of her face, and the strange expression resulting from her state of mind, added to her beauty, but to me they were unmistakable signs that her future was an early death.

Gimmerton church bells were still ringing, and the murmur of the little stream in the valley came sweetly to the ear. Catherine seemed to be listening, but she had the dreamy look that I have mentioned.

'There's a letter for you, Mrs Linton,' I said, gently placing it in her hand. 'You must read it now, because it needs an answer. Shall I open it?'

'Yes,' she answered, without changing the direction of her eyes.

I did so, and gave it to her. She pulled away her hand and let it fall.

I replaced it on her knee, and stood waiting.

At last I said, 'Must I read it? It is from Mr Heathcliff.'

There was a sudden movement, and a troubled flash of memory, and a struggle to arrange her ideas. She lifted the letter and seemed to read it, and when she came to the name at the end she breathed in deeply: but still I found she had not understood its meaning. She pointed to the name, and fixed her eyes on me with sad and questioning eagerness.

'He wishes to see you,' I said. 'He's probably in the garden by this time and impatient to know your answer.'

As I spoke, I noticed a large dog lying outside on the sunny grass below. It raised its ears and then, smoothing them back, showed by a movement of the tail that someone was coming whom it did not consider a stranger. Mrs Linton leant forward and listened breathlessly.

A step was heard in the hall. With indescribable eagerness Catherine directed her eyes towards the entrance to her room. In a moment Heathcliff was at her side and had her in his arms.

He neither spoke nor loosened his hold for several minutes. I saw he could hardly bear, for pure misery, to look into her face! He felt, from the moment he saw her, that there was no hope that she would recover. Her future was decided; she was sure to die.

'Oh, Cathy! Oh, my life! How can I bear it?' was the first sentence he spoke. And now he looked at her so deeply that I thought it would bring tears to his eyes; but they burned with pain, they did not melt.

'What now?' said Catherine, leaning back, and returning his look with one of sudden anger. 'You and Edgar have broken my heart, Heathcliff! I shall not pity you, not I. You have killed me – and are stronger for it, I think. How many years do you intend to live after I am gone?'

Heathcliff had knelt on one knee. He attempted to rise, but she seized his hair and kept him down.

'Oh why can't I hold you,' she continued bitterly, 'until we are both dead? I wouldn't care what you suffered. Why shouldn't you suffer? I do! Will you forget me? Will you be happy when I am in the earth?'

'Don't make me as mad as yourself!' he cried, forcing his head free. 'Are you possessed by a devil, to talk like that when you are dying? Do you realize that all those words will be burned into my memory? You know that it is not true that I have killed you: and Catherine, you know that I could as easily forget you as my own existence! Is it not enough for your cursed selfishness that while you are at peace I shall be in misery?'

'I shall not be at peace,' murmured Catherine, brought back to a sense of weakness by the violent, irregular beating of her heart.

She said no more until the attack was over, then she continued, more kindly: 'I'm not wishing you greater pain than I have, Heathcliff. I only wish us never to be parted: and if the memory of any word of mine should give you pain in the future, think that I feel the same pain beneath the earth, and forgive me! Come here and kneel down again! You have never harmed me in your life.'

Heathcliff went to the back of her chair and leaned over, but not far enough to let her see his face, which was deathly white. She bent round to look at him; he would not allow it. Turning quickly he walked to the fireplace, where he stood silent with his back towards us. Catherine looked at him, then after a pause she spoke to me in an offended voice.

'You see, Nelly, he will not give way for a moment. That is how I'm loved. Well, never mind. That is not my Heathcliff. I shall love mine still. I am surprised he won't be near me,' she went on to herself. 'I thought he wished it. Heathcliff, dear, do come to me.'

In her eagerness she rose and supported herself on the arm of the chair. At that request he turned to her, looking completely miserable. For a moment they stayed apart. Then Catherine seemed to jump, and he caught her and held her tightly. I thought she had fainted but, when I approached to see, he turned on me and pulled her closer to him, half mad with jealousy, so I stood to one side, not knowing what to do.

Soon a movement of Catherine's made me feel a little happier. She put her hand to his neck to bring his cheek to hers, while he said wildly: 'You teach me how cruel you've been — cruel and false! Why did you scorn me? Why were you false to your own heart, Cathy? I have not one word of comfort. You deserve this! You have killed yourself. Yes, you may kiss me, and cry, and force me to do the same — it is your punishment. You loved me — then how *could* you leave me? Because misery, degradation and death could not part us, *you* did it! I have not broken your heart – you have broken it, and in breaking it, you have broken mine. It is worse for me that I am strong. Do I want to live? Would *you* want to live with your soul in the grave?'

'Leave me alone,' cried Catherine. 'If I've done wrong, I'm dying for it. You left me too, but I forgive you. Forgive me!'

'It is hard, but I forgive you what you have done to me. I love my murderer – but yours! How can I?'

They were silent, their faces hidden against each other and washed by each other's tears. I became very uncomfortable, as the afternoon was passing and I could see in the sunshine up the valley a crowd of people outside the church.

'The service is over,' I said. 'Master will be here in half an hour.'

Heathcliff cursed and pulled Catherine closer. She never moved.

Soon I saw a group of the servants coming up the road.

Then Edgar Linton opened the gate and walked through.

'Now he's here,' I cried.

'I must go, Cathy,' said Heathcliff, 'but, as sure as I'm alive, I'll see you again before you are asleep. I shall be near your window.'

'You must not go!' she answered, holding him as firmly as her strength allowed.

'For one hour!' he begged.

'Not for one minute,' she replied.

'I must. Linton will be up immediately.'

He wanted to rise, but she hung on to him tightly. There was madness in her face. 'No! Oh, don't, don't go. It is the last time.'

Heathcliff murmured a curse on Edgar, and sank back into his seat.

'Quiet, my dearest! I'll stay. If he shot me now, I'd die happy.'

I heard my master coming up the stairs.

'She doesn't know what she says!' I cried. 'Will you ruin her, because she has not sense enough to help herself? Get up! We are all finished!'

Mr Linton heard the noise and came faster. I saw that Catherine's arms had fallen, and her head hung down.   .

'Either she's fainted or she's dead!' I thought.

Edgar jumped on his uninvited guest, white with shock and anger. I cannot tell what he intended to do, but the other stopped him by placing the lifeless-looking form in his arms.

'Unless you are a devil,' he said, 'help her first — then speak to me.'

6   *The Taming of the Shrew*
from *More Tales from Shakespeare*
Charles and Mary Lamb

William Shakespeare (1564–1616) was born in Stratford-upon-Avon, and by 1592 he was famous in London as an actor and writer. Over the next twenty years he wrote thirty-eight plays; most of these are considered to be masterpieces. He also wrote a lot of great poetry. Four hundred years later, he is still the most popular and famous writer in the English language.

In 1807 Charles Lamb and his sister, Mary Lamb, were asked to write the stories from the best known of Shakespeare's plays in a way that children could easily understand. Their adaptations of the stories were a great success.

In the early comedy *The Taming of the Shrew* (first performed in 1594) Petruchio, a visitor from Verona in search of a rich wife, marries Katharine, the bad-tempered daughter of a rich gentleman from Padua. Petruchio pays no attention to Katharine's rudeness, and enjoys destroying her spirit and making her an obedient wife.

Petruchio behaves very badly to Katharine during their wedding, and refuses to stay for the expensive meal provided by her father. In this extract, Petruchio and Katharine have just arrived home after a long, uncomfortable journey on horseback.

Petruchio welcomed her kindly to her home, but he had made up his mind that she should have neither food nor rest that night. The tables were spread and supper soon served, but Petruchio pretended to find something wrong with every dish. He threw the meat on the floor, and ordered the servants to take it away. All this he did, as he said, in love for his Katharine, so that she did not have to eat meat that was not well cooked. And when Katharine went to rest, tired and supperless, he found something wrong with the bed; he threw the bedclothes around the room so that she was forced to sit down in a chair. If she fell asleep, she was quickly woken up by her husband's loud voice, as he shouted at the servants for making his wife's marriage bed so badly.

The next day Petruchio continued to act in the same way. He still spoke kind words to Katharine, but when she attempted to eat, he found something wrong with everything that was put in front of her and threw the breakfast on the floor as he had done the supper. Katharine, proud Katharine, was forced to beg the servants to bring her food secretly, but they had already been given their orders by Petruchio and replied that they dared not give her anything without their master's knowledge.

'Oh!' Katharine said to herself. 'Did he marry me to keep me hungry? Poor people that come to my father's door are given food. But I, who never had to beg for anything, am kept without food and without sleep. He keeps me awake and feeds me with his shouting. And the thing that makes me more angry is that he does it all in the name of perfect love.'

Her thoughts were interrupted by the entrance of Petruchio. He had brought her a small piece of meat, and he said to her, 'How is my sweet Kate? See, love, how much I think of you. I have cooked your meat myself. I am sure this kindness deserves thanks. What, not a word? Then you do not love the meat, and all

the trouble I have taken is for nothing.' He then ordered the
servant to take the dish away.

Her great hunger had lessened Katharine's pride and, though
she was still very angry, she said, 'I beg you, leave it here.'

But Petruchio intended to make her obey him more than this,
and he replied, 'The poorest service is repaid with thanks, and so
shall mine before you touch the meat.'

So Katharine said with difficulty, 'I thank you, sir.'

7   *Dr Zhivago*   Boris Pasternak

Boris Pasternak (1890–1960) was born in Moscow. He wrote
poetry and stories during the 1920s and 1930s, but he was not
accepted as an official 'Soviet writer', and none of his work was
published between 1933 and 1943.

Dr Zhivago is Pasternak's most important work, and is one of
the greatest love stories of the twentieth century. The
government did not allow it to be published in the USSR, but it
appeared in Italy in 1957 and won the Nobel Prize for Literature
in 1958. Because of his problems with the Soviet government,
Pasternak refused to accept the prize.

Dr Zhivago is about the struggle of ordinary people in a
violently unstable world, but it is, above all, a love story. Yury
Zhivago and Lara Antipova are strongly attracted to each other,
although they are both already married. Nothing makes sense
about their love, but nothing makes any sense without it, and
they allow it to govern their lives. The dream that one day they
will be together helps them to overcome the horrors of physical
reality – war, revolution, poverty and illness.

In this extract Zhivago has moved from Moscow with his
wife, Tonya, and his family to Varykino, an estate in the Urals near
the town of Yuryatin. He has not seen Lara for more than two

years, since they worked together as doctor and nurse in the last days of the war.

Zhivago sees Lara again

One morning Yury was sitting in his usual seat in the library's reading room. He had a large pile of books on the table in front of him and was surrounded by other regular library users. He was ready for several hours of hard work.

He was concentrating on his books when he noticed a change in the room. At the far end there was a new reader. Yury immediately recognized Nurse Antipova. She was sitting with her back to him, speaking in a low voice to one of the women who worked in the reading room. This woman had looked ill all morning, but after whispering to Lara for a few minutes, she walked back to her desk smiling and looking very much improved. Several people noticed the change in the sick woman and looked up and smiled at Lara, but she was already lost in the book she was reading.

Yury wanted to go and speak to her, but he felt shy and did not want to interrupt her work. He turned away from her and tried to read his own books, but he kept thinking of her. Suddenly he knew that the calm, beautiful voice that had come to him in his dreams was hers.

'She does not try to please people or to look beautiful, but that makes her lovelier than ever,' he thought. 'How well she does everything! She makes reading look so simple, a thing that even animals could do.' He looked at her and felt completely peaceful. Then he went back to his studies with a smile on his lips.

After reading for several hours, Yury decided to speak to Lara, but when he looked up he found that she had left the library. He returned his books to the desk and accidentally saw a form with Lara's name and address on it. It wasn't many days before Yury went looking for her house.

The house was not difficult to find. Yury opened the gate and saw Lara fetching water. She looked amazed but remained natural in her manner. All she said was: 'Zhivago!'

'Larissa Fyodorovna!' whispered Yury.

'What are you doing here? Have you come to see me?' Lara asked.

'Who else?'

'Why didn't you speak to me in the library? I know you saw me.'

They walked into Lara's small flat like two old friends. They drank tea, talked about their children and discussed the revolution. Yury told Lara about meeting Strelnikov.

'You saw him!' Lara said in amazement. 'How extraordinary! What kind of impression did he make on you?'

'On the whole, very good. I think he is a brilliant man, one of a kind. He will be very important for the country, but, for some reason, I think he will fail in the end.'

'I must be honest with you before you say anything else. The Strelnikov you met is my husband, Pasha Antipov.'

'He can't be,' cried Yury. 'What do you have in common with such a man?'

'I don't understand everything he is doing, but I know that he believes in his goals. Maybe you think he doesn't love Katya and me, that he has forgotten us? Well, you are wrong. Someday he will be finished with fighting. Then he will come home to us and lay his victories at my feet.'

Just then Katya came in from school. Lara surprised the eight-year-old by lifting her up and holding her tightly. . . .

. . . Two months later Yury was riding home from Yuryatin. For those two months he had been deceiving Tonya, lying to her about why he needed to stay some nights every week in Yuryatin. He had never chosen between Tonya and Lara. He still loved his wife and did not want to hurt her in any way. At home he felt

26

like a criminal. He knew he was putting his family's happiness and safety at risk.

But now things would change. He had decided to tell Tonya everything and beg her to forgive him. He had told Lara that afternoon that he could not continue to be unfaithful to Tonya. Lara had listened calmly and agreed with Yury as tears rolled down her cheeks.

Yury was thinking about Lara and desperately wanted to see her again. He hadn't said anything to Tonya yet, so why couldn't he see Lara just one more time? He would make sure that she understood how much he truly loved her, and he would again explain, more gently this time, why he had to stop seeing her.

The thought of seeing Lara again made Yury's heart jump with happiness. He was picturing his next visit to her house when he heard a gun fired very close to him. Three men on horses stood in his path.

'Don't move, Comrade Doctor,' said the oldest of the three. 'If you obey orders, you will be perfectly safe. If you don't, it's very simple: we'll shoot you. Our army needs a doctor and you've been chosen. Now, follow us.'

8 *Pride and Prejudice* Jane Austen

Jane Austen (1775–1817) had an unexciting life, and her novels were not especially popular in her lifetime. But she had some important admirers, including Sir Walter Scott, the novelist. Her best known novels include *Sense and Sensibility* (1811), *Pride and Prejudice* (1813), *Emma* (1816) and *Persuasion* (1818).

Pride and Prejudice is a story about middle-class, provincial people, and their constant interest in courtship and marriage. Mrs Bennet's only aim in life is to find suitable husbands for her five daughters. She is delighted when her wealthy neighbour, Charles

Bingley, falls in love with her eldest daughter, Jane. Bingley's even wealthier friend, FitzWilliam Darcy, considers himself socially superior to the Bennet family. He tries to persuade Bingley to stop seeing Jane, but soon finds himself in love with Jane's younger sister, Elizabeth, instead.

In this extract, Darcy confesses his true feelings for Elizabeth.

Darcy declares his love for Elizabeth

Elizabeth was suddenly interrupted by the sound of the doorbell and, to her complete astonishment, she saw Mr Darcy walk into the room. In a hurried manner he immediately began to ask after her health. She answered him with cold politeness. He sat down for a few minutes and then, getting up, walked around the room. Elizabeth was surprised, but did not say a word. After a silence of several minutes, he came towards her in a troubled manner and began to speak:

'I have struggled without success. My feelings will not be controlled. You must allow me to tell you how warmly I admire and love you.'

Elizabeth's astonishment was beyond expression. She looked away, red in the face, and was silent. He considered this enough encouragement, and the expression of all that he felt for her immediately followed.

He spoke well. But there were other feelings to be described besides those of his heart, and his words were more concerned with pride than love. His sense of her inferiority, his feelings that he was lowering himself, the family considerations that had caused his judgement to oppose his preference, all were expressed with a force that was unlikely to make his offer acceptable.

In spite of her dislike, she could not fail to realize what an honour it was to receive such a man's attention. And though her intentions did not change for one moment, she was at first sorry for the pain he would receive until, insulted by his language as he continued, she lost all pity in anger. She tried to control herself, so she could answer him patiently when he had finished. He ended by expressing the hope that he would now be rewarded by her acceptance of his hand in marriage. As he said this, she could clearly see that he had no doubt that she would accept his offer. Such confidence could only increase her annoyance, and when he had ended, the colour in her face deepened and she said:

'If I could feel grateful, as I believe one should in such a situation, I would now thank you. But I cannot – I have never desired your good opinion, and you have certainly given it most unwillingly. The reasons which, you tell me, have prevented the expression of your feelings until now, can have little difficulty in bringing them under control.'

Mr Darcy, whose eyes were fixed on her face, seemed to hear her words with no less anger than surprise. He became pale, and the confusion in his mind was plain in every feature. Finally, in a voice of forced calmness, he said:

'And this is all the reply which I am to have the honour of expecting! I might, perhaps, wish to be informed why, with so little attempt at politeness, I am refused.'

'I might as well ask,' she replied, 'why, with so clear an intention of insulting me, you chose to tell me that you liked me against your will. Was that not some excuse for impoliteness, if I was impolite? But I have other reasons. Do you think that anything would lead me to accept the man who has been responsible for ruining, perhaps for ever, the happiness of my dear sister?'

As she spoke these words, Mr Darcy's face changed colour, but he listened without interrupting her while she continued:

'Nothing can excuse the unfair and ungenerous part that you played there. You cannot deny that you have been responsible for dividing the pair of them.'

She paused, and saw that he was listening in a manner that proved he did not understand her anger.

'Is it not true that you have done it?' she repeated.

He then replied with calmness: 'Yes, it is true that I did everything in my power to separate my friend from your sister, and that I am glad of my success. I have been kinder towards him than towards myself.'

Elizabeth appeared not to notice this polite remark, but its meaning did not escape her, and it was not likely to soften her feelings.

'But it is not only this affair,' she continued, 'on which my dislike is based. Long before, your character was made plain in the story which I received many months ago from Mr Wickham.'

'You take an eager interest in that gentleman's concerns,' said Darcy, in a more troubled voice, and with deeper colour in his face.

'No one who knows his misfortunes can help feeling an interest in him.'

'His misfortunes!' repeated Darcy scornfully. 'Yes, his misfortunes have been great.'

'And you are responsible,' cried Elizabeth with energy. '*You* have reduced him to his present state.'

'And this,' cried Darcy, as he walked with quick steps across the room, 'is your opinion of me. I thank you for explaining it so fully. But perhaps,' he added, stopping in his walk, and turning towards her, 'these offences would have been forgiven if your pride had not been hurt by my honest explanation of the reasons that made me wait so long. I am not ashamed of the feelings that I expressed. They were natural and fair. Could you expect me to be happy about the inferiority of your relations?'

Elizabeth felt herself becoming more angry every moment, but she tried to speak calmly as she said:

'Even if you had offered me your hand in a polite manner, I would never have accepted it.'

Again his astonishment was clear. She went on:

'From the beginning, your manners struck me as showing the greatest pride in yourself and scorn for the feelings of others, and I had not known you a month before I felt that you were the last person in the world whom I could ever be persuaded to marry.'

'You have said quite enough, madam. Forgive me for wasting so much of your time, and accept my best wishes for your health and happiness.'

And with these words he quickly left the room.

The disorder of Elizabeth's mind was now painfully great, and from actual weakness she sat down and cried for half an hour.

◆

Elizabeth begins to return Darcy's love but Lady Catherine de Bourgh, Darcy's formidable aunt, strongly disapproves of their relationship. In this extract she visits Elizabeth.

Lady Catherine de Bourgh visits Elizabeth

One morning, about a week later, a carriage suddenly appeared outside the house. It was too early for visitors, and neither the carriage nor the uniform of the servant was familiar. The two lovers [Elizabeth's sister, Jane, and Mr Bingley] immediately escaped to the garden, leaving the rest of the ladies to guess who the stranger could be, until the door was thrown open and Lady Catherine de Bourgh entered.

She walked in, looking more unpleasant than usual, made no other reply to Elizabeth's greeting than a slight movement of the head, and sat down without a word.

After sitting for a moment in silence, she said, very stiffly, to Elizabeth:

'I hope you are well, Miss Bennet. That lady, I suppose, is your mother?'

Elizabeth replied shortly that she was.

'And *that*, I suppose, is one of your sisters?'

'Yes, madam,' replied Mrs Bennet, to whom Elizabeth had mentioned the visitor's name, and who was feeling highly honoured by her coming.

'You have a very small park, here,' observed Lady Catherine, after a short silence, 'and this must be a most inconvenient sitting room for the evening in summer. The windows appear to be facing west.'

Mrs Bennet informed her that they never sat there after dinner, and then added:

'May I ask whether you left Mr and Mrs Collins well?'

'Yes, very well.'

Elizabeth now expected that she would produce a letter for her from Charlotte, because it seemed the only likely reason for her visit. But no letter appeared, and she could not understand the visit at all.

Mrs Bennet, with great politeness, begged Lady Catherine to have something to eat or drink, but this was firmly, and not very politely, refused. Then, rising, Lady Catherine said to Elizabeth: 'Miss Bennet, I should be glad to take a walk in your garden, if you will give me your company.'

Elizabeth obeyed. As they passed through the hall, Lady Catherine opened the doors of the other rooms, and announced that they were quite a good size.

They walked in silence towards the little wood. Elizabeth had decided to make no effort at conversation with a woman who was now more than usually rude and unpleasant. As soon as they entered the wood, Lady Catherine began in the following manner:

'You can have no difficulty, Miss Bennet, in understanding the reason for my visit. Your own heart, your own conscience must tell you why I have come.'

Elizabeth looked at her in astonishment.

'Miss Bennet,' she continued in an angry voice, 'you ought to know that I will not be treated without proper respect for my position. A report of a most upsetting nature reached me two days ago. I was told that you, Miss Elizabeth Bennet, would in all probability be soon united to my nephew, my own nephew. Though I *know* that it must be a shameful lie, I immediately decided to come here so that I could make my feelings known to you.'

'If you believed it was impossible,' said Elizabeth, her face turning red with astonishment and scorn, 'I am surprised that you took the trouble of coming so far.'

'I find your attitude unpleasant, Miss Bennet. I will be satisfied. Has he, has my nephew, made you an offer of marriage?'

'You have said that it is impossible.'

'Miss Bennet, do you know who I am? Let me be rightly understood. Mr Darcy is engaged to my daughter. Now, what have you to say?'

'Only this – that if it is true, you can have no reason to suppose that he will make an offer to me.'

Lady Catherine paused for a moment, and then replied:

'The arrangement between them is of a special kind. From their childhood they have been intended for each other. It was the favourite wish of his mother, as well as of myself. Have you no respect for the wishes of his relations?'

'But how does that affect me? If Mr Darcy wishes, may he not make another choice? And if I am that choice, why may I not accept him?'

'I will not be interrupted! Hear me in silence. I see there is a seat over there. Let us sit down. My daughter and my nephew are made for each other. Their birth and their fortunes are noble. And what will divide them? The plans of a young woman without status or money?'

'Your nephew is a gentleman, and I am a gentleman's daughter.'

'But what is your mother? Who are your uncles and aunts? Do you imagine that I am without knowledge of their condition?'

'If your nephew does not complain about them,' replied Elizabeth, 'it can be nothing to you.'

'Tell me, are you engaged to him?'

Elizabeth could only say: 'I am not.' Lady Catherine seemed pleased.

'And will you promise never to become engaged to my nephew?'

'I will make no promise of any kind.'

'Miss Bennet, I am shocked. The facts concerning your younger sister are fully known to me. Can I allow such a girl to be my nephew's sister? Can I allow *her* husband, the son of his father's servant, to be his brother?'

'You can now have nothing more to say to me,' Elizabeth answered with bitterness. 'You have insulted me in every possible way. I must beg you to return to the house.'

She rose as she spoke. Lady Catherine also rose, highly angered. She talked on, threatening to punish Elizabeth if she did not change her mind. Then, when they were at the door of her carriage, Lady Catherine suddenly turned round and added:

'I leave you without a goodbye, Miss Bennet. I send no greetings to your mother. You do not deserve such attention. I am most seriously displeased.'

Elizabeth made no answer, but walked quietly into the house.

9   The Hound of the Baskervilles
Sir Arthur Conan Doyle

Sir Arthur Conan Doyle (1859–1930) created Sherlock Holmes, the world's most famous fictional detective. The first Holmes mystery, *A Study in Scarlet*, appeared in 1887. Conan Doyle wrote fifty-six short stories and four novels about Holmes and his friend and colleague, Dr Watson.

The Hound of the Baskervilles (1902) is the most famous of the novels. One night Sir Charles Baskerville is found dead just outside his home, Baskerville Hall. Many of the Baskerville family have died mysteriously. It is widely believed that they were murdered by a large, evil hound. Sherlock Holmes is called to solve the mystery and to save the new owner of Baskerville Hall from a terrible death.

Holmes is not the sort of man to experience any of life's great passions himself, so he is perhaps a good person to solve crimes committed by people who do. He also knows how to use a person's emotions – in this case, wounded love – to discover useful information. In this extract, Holmes interviews Mrs Laura Lyons about her role in the death of Sir Charles Baskerville.

Sherlock Holmes interviews Mrs Lyons

Mrs Laura Lyons was in her room, and Sherlock Holmes began the conversation with a directness that surprised her.

'You have confessed that you asked Sir Charles to be at the gate in the Yew Avenue at ten o'clock. We know that that was the place and time of his death. You have not admitted what the connection is between those events.'

'There is no connection.'

'That is very strange! I wish to be perfectly honest with you, Mrs Lyons. We consider this to be a case of murder, and it may involve not only your friend, Mr Stapleton, but his wife as well.'

The lady jumped up from her chair. 'His wife!' she cried.

'The fact is no longer a secret. The person he calls his sister is really his wife.'

'His wife!' she said again. 'He is not a married man. Prove it to me. And if you can do so – !' The angry flash of her eyes said more than any words.

'I have come ready to do so,' said Holmes, taking several papers from his pocket. 'Here is a photograph of the two of them, taken in York four years ago. On the back is written: "Mr and Mrs Vandeleur", but you will have no difficulty in recognizing him – and her also, if you know what she looks like. Here are three written descriptions by honest witnesses of Mr and Mrs Vandeleur, who at that time kept St Oliver's private school. Read them, and see what opinion you form.'

She looked quickly at them, and then said, with the face of a desperate woman: 'Mr Holmes, this man had offered me marriage on condition that I could get a divorce from my husband. He has lied to me. I see now that I was only a tool in his hands. Why should I be true to him, who has never been with me? Why should I try to protect him from the results of his own evil acts? Ask me what you like, I will tell you everything. I promise that when I wrote the letter I never dreamed of any harm coming to the old gentleman, who was my kindest friend.'

'I believe you. Did Stapleton suggest writing the letter?'

'Yes. He told me what to write.'

'Did he say that you would receive help from Sir Charles with the money needed for your divorce?'

'Exactly.'

'Then after you had sent the letter, did he persuade you not to keep the appointment?'

'Yes. He told me that it would hurt his pride if any other man gave me money for such a purpose.'

36

'Did he later make you promise to say nothing about your appointment with Sir Charles?'

'He did. He said that I should certainly be suspected if the facts became known. He frightened me into remaining silent.'

'I think that you have had a fortunate escape. You have had him in your power and he knew it, but you are still alive. Good morning, Mrs Lyons.'

10   *Jude the Obscure*   Thomas Hardy

Thomas Hardy (1840–1928) grew up in the south-west of England and worked there as an architect before moving to London. There, he became a professional writer. One of his early books was *Under the Greenwood Tree* (1872), soon followed by *Far from the Madding Crowd* (1874). Other novels, all set in the south-west of England, include *The Mayor of Casterbridge* (1886) and *Tess of the D'Urbevilles* (1891).

Jude the Obscure (1896) was Hardy's last novel. Many readers were shocked by the pessimistic description of the 'war between flesh and spirit' in the story. After he has been trapped into marriage by Arabella Donn, Jude meets and is immediately attracted to his intelligent but unstable cousin, Sue Bridehead. This love will have a tragic effect on both their lives. In this extract, Jude has a secret meeting with Sue, who is now married to his former teacher, Mr Phillotson.

Jude has a secret meeting with Sue

Jude climbed up from the station to the hilltop town of Shaston and found the schoolroom empty. Mr Phillotson was away at a meeting, said a girl cleaning the floor, but Mrs Phillotson would be back in a few minutes.

There was a piano in the room, the same piano that Phillotson had had at Marygreen. Jude, as he waited, played a song he had heard at a church in Melchester.

Lightly, someone touched his left hand. 'I like that song,' said Sue. 'I learnt it at the training college.'

'Then you play it for me.'

Sue sat down and played. When she had finished, they again touched hands.

'We'll have some tea,' Sue said quickly. 'Are you still studying Theology?'

'Yes, harder than ever.'

'I could come and see you at one of your churches next week.'

'No. Don't come!'

'What have I done? I thought we two . . .'

'Sue, I sometimes think you're playing with my feelings,' Jude said angrily.

She jumped up. 'Oh, Jude, that was a cruel thing to say! Some women need love so much, and they may not be able to give their love to the person they are married to! But you're too honest to understand . . . Now you must go. I'm sorry my husband's not at home.'

'Are you?' Jude went out.

'Jude! Jude!' Sue called pitifully from the window. 'I'm really all alone! Come and see me again. Come next week.'

'All right,' said Jude . . .

. . . Two days later, Sue changed her mind. 'Don't come next week,' she wrote to Jude. 'We were too free. You must try to forget me.'

'You're right,' Jude wrote back. 'It's a lesson I ought to learn at this Easter season.'

Their decision seemed final, but on Easter Monday Drusilla Fawley died and it was necessary to inform Sue. 'Aunt Drusilla is dead,' he wrote from Marygreen. 'She will be buried on Friday afternoon.'

Sue came, alone and nervous, and the cousins went together to the burial service.

'She was always against marriage, wasn't she?' asked Sue afterwards, when they were back at the familiar cottage.

'Yes. Particularly for members of our family.'

Sue looked at Jude. 'Would a woman be very bad, do you think, if she didn't like living with her husband just because she had, well, a physical feeling against it?'

Jude looked away. 'Sue, you're not happy in your marriage, are you?'

'Of course I am!... But I have to go back by the six o'clock train.'

'That train won't take you to Shaston. You'll have to stay here until tomorrow. Mrs Edlin has a room if you don't wish to stay in this house.'

Sue's hand lay on the tea-table. Jude put his hand on it, but Sue took hers away. 'That's silly, Sue!' he cried. 'It was a totally innocent action!'

'Then I must tell Richard that you hold my hand,' she said. 'Unless you are sure that you mean it only as my cousin.'

'Absolutely sure. I have no feelings of love now.'

'Oh! How has that happened?'

'I saw Arabella when I was at Christminster.'

'So she's come back and you never told me! I suppose you'll live with her now?'

'Of course – just as you live with your husband.'

There were tears in Sue's eyes. 'How could your heart go back to Arabella so soon?... But I must be as honest with you as you've been with me. Though I like Mr Phillotson as a friend, I hate living with him as a husband! There, now I've told you.' She bent her face down into her hands and cried until the little table shook.

'I *thought* there was something wrong, Sue.'

'There's nothing wrong, except the awful contract to give myself to this man whenever he wishes. *He* does nothing wrong, except that he has become a little cold since he found out my feelings. That's why he didn't come today. Oh, I'm so unhappy! Don't come near me, Jude. You mustn't!'

But Jude had jumped up and put his face against hers. 'It all happened because I was married before we met, didn't it? That's the only reason you became *his* wife, Sue, isn't it?'

Instead of replying, Sue left the house and went across to Mrs Edlin's cottage ...

... Next morning, Jude walked with Sue as far as the main road to Alfredston. He must not kiss her goodbye, she said, unless he promised that he kissed her only as a cousin and a friend. No, he would not promise that. So they separated. But then both looked round at the same time – and ran back into each other's arms, kissing close and long.

The kiss was an important moment for Jude. To him it seemed the purest moment of his life, but to his Church it would not seem like that. He realized that he could not possibly continue in his forbidden love for Sue *and* hope to become a teacher of religion.

That evening he lit a fire in the garden and calmly put all his theological books onto the flames.

11   *Much Ado About Nothing*
from *Tales from Shakespeare*
Charles and Mary Lamb

William Shakespeare (1564–1616) was born in Stratford-upon-Avon, and by 1592 he was famous in London as an actor and writer. Over the next twenty years he wrote thirty-eight plays; most of these are considered to be masterpieces. He also wrote a lot of great poetry. Four hundred years later, he is still the most popular and famous writer in the English language.

In 1807 Charles Lamb and his sister, Mary Lamb, were asked to write the stories from the best known of Shakespeare's plays in a way that children could easily understand. Their adaptations of the stories were a great success.

First performed in 1598, *Much Ado About Nothing* shows Shakespeare's skill at presenting secondary characters. Benedick, a lord of Padua, and Beatrice, the niece of Leonato, the Governor of Messina, seem to dislike each other. They are always fighting. In this extract their friends (Prince Pedro of Aragon, Leonato, Claudio, a lord of Florence, and Hero, Beatrice's cousin) try to stop their constant fighting by playing a trick on them, with surprising results.

Benedick and Beatrice

The prince had a plan. The gentlemen should make Benedick believe that Beatrice was in love with him, and Hero should make Beatrice believe that Benedick was in love with her.

The prince, Leonato and Claudio started work first. Finding their opportunity when Benedick was quietly reading in the garden, the prince and his helpers took their position among the trees. They were so near that Benedick could not help hearing all they said. After some talk on other subjects, the prince said, 'Tell me, Leonato. What did you say to me the other day — that your niece Beatrice was in love with Benedick? I did not think that lady would know how to love any man.'

'No, nor I, my lord,' answered Leonato. 'It is interesting that she should love Benedick so much, when she always seems to dislike him.'

Claudio then said that Hero had told him Beatrice was in love with Benedick. She loved him so much that she would certainly die of sadness if he could not be persuaded to love her. However, Leonato and Claudio seemed to agree that this was impossible because Benedick had always spoken against all attractive ladies, and especially against Beatrice.

The prince pretended to feel great pity for Beatrice as he listened to this, and he said, 'It would be good if Benedick were told about this.'

'Why?' said Claudio. 'He would only make fun of her, and upset the poor lady even more.'

'And if he did,' said the prince, 'he would be in trouble. Beatrice is a lovely lady, and very wise in everything except in loving Benedick.'

Then the prince signalled to his companions that they should walk, and leave Benedick to think about what he had heard. . . .

. . . Benedick had been listening with great eagerness to this conversation; and when he heard Beatrice loved him, he said to himself, 'Is it possible? Can it be true? Is that the way the wind blows?'

And when they had gone, he thought:

'This cannot be a trick! They were very serious, and they have the truth from Hero and seem to pity the lady. Love me! Then her love must be returned! I never thought I would marry. But they say the lady is lovely – and wise in everything except loving me. Well, that is no great proof of her foolishness. But here comes Beatrice. Yes, it is true, she is an attractive lady.'

Beatrice now came towards him, and said with her usual sharpness, 'I have been sent against my will to ask you to come in to dinner.'

Benedick, who had never felt himself able to speak so politely to her before, replied, 'Fair Beatrice, I thank you for your trouble.' When Beatrice left him, after two or three more rude remarks, Benedick thought he had noticed a hidden kindness under her hard words, and he said to himself, 'If I do not take pity on her and love her, I am an evil man.' . . .

. . . Since the gentleman was now caught in the net they had spread for him, it was Hero's turn to play her part with Beatrice. And for this purpose she sent for Ursula and Margaret, two women who served her, and she said to Margaret, 'Good Margaret, run to the sitting room; there you will find my cousin Beatrice talking to the prince and Claudio. Whisper in her ear that Ursula and I are walking in the garden, and that we are talking about her. Tell her to come and listen.'

'I will make her come immediately, I promise you,' said Margaret.

Hero then took Ursula with her into the garden, and said to her, 'Now, Ursula, when Beatrice comes, we will walk up and down this path, and our conversation will only be about Benedick, and when I name him, you must praise him more than any man has ever deserved. I shall be telling you that Benedick is in love with Beatrice. Now begin – look over there where Beatrice is running towards us to hear our conversation.'

They then began. Hero appeared to answer something which Ursula had said: 'No, truly, Ursula. She is too proud; she is as shy as a wild bird.'

'But are you sure,' said Ursula, 'that Signor* Benedick loves Beatrice so completely?'

'The prince says so,' Hero replied. 'And my lord Claudio. They begged me to tell her; but I persuaded them, if they loved Benedick, never to let Beatrice know of it.'

'Certainly,' replied Ursula, 'it would not be a good thing for her to know about his love, in case she made fun of it.'

'Exactly,' said Hero. 'I have never yet seen a man, wise, young, or beautiful, whom she would not criticize.'

'Such cruel judgements are not good,' said Ursula.

'No,' replied Hero, 'but who would dare to tell her so? If I spoke, she would just laugh at me.'

*Signor: the Italian word for Mr

'Oh, you wrong your cousin,' said Ursula. 'She cannot refuse a gentleman as fine as Signor Benedick.'

'He has an excellent name,' said Hero. 'In fact, he is the first man in Italy, except for my dear Claudio.'

Hero then told Ursula that she was going to be married to Claudio the next day, and asked her to go in with her and look at some new clothes, as she wished to ask her advice about what she should wear.

When they went away, Beatrice, who had been listening very eagerly to this talk, cried out, 'Can this be true? Benedick, love on! I will repay you, and soften my wild heart under your loving hand.'

12   *Jane Eyre*   Charlotte Brontë

Charlotte Brontë (1816–55) was the third of six children in a family of writers. After the deaths of two of her sisters, Maria and Elizabeth, Charlotte lived at home with her other sisters, Emily and Anne. The three girls educated themselves and saw little of other families. To make their quiet village life more interesting, Charlotte encouraged her sisters to invent stories.

Jane Eyre was published in 1847, the same year as Emily's *Wuthering Heights* and Anne's *Agnes Grey*. Her other novels include *Shirley* (1849), *Villette* (1853) and *The Professor* (1857).

Jane Eyre is a story, narrated by Jane herself, about a young woman from a poor background who struggles to make a life for herself, and at the same time to obey her own principles. In this extract, Jane has gone to Thornfield Hall to work as a governess. One evening, she offers to deliver a letter to the village, a few kilometres away. On the way, she sits on a stile to listen to the soft murmur of streams in the fields and valleys.

A loud noise interrupted these murmurings: a sound of heavy steps on the bridge. A horse was coming; it was still hidden by a bend in the path, but it was close now. I was just leaving the stile; as the path was narrow, though, I sat still to let the horse go by. All sorts of thoughts, bright and dark, came into my mind, including troubling memories of childhood stories. I remembered some of Bessie's stories of a ghost which took the form of a horse or dog and was seen in lonely places.

The horse was very near, but not yet in sight, when I heard a movement in the bushes, and a great dog with a black and white coat ran by. It was a lion-like creature with long hair and a large head. The horse followed – a tall animal with a rider on its back. He passed, and I went on a few steps, then I turned. The sound of something falling had suddenly attracted my attention. Man and horse were down; they had slipped on a sheet of ice. The dog came running back and, seeing his master in difficulty, came to me for help. I walked down to the traveller, who was by this time struggling to free himself from his horse.

'Are you injured, sir?'

I think he was swearing. He did not reply directly.

'Can I do anything?' I asked again.

'You must just stand to one side,' he answered as he rose, first to his knees, then to his feet. The horse was raised, the dog silenced with the command 'Down, Pilot!' The traveller now, bending down, felt his boot and leg, then sat down on the stile from which I had just risen.

'If you are hurt and want help, sir, I can get someone from Thornfield Hall.'

'Thank you. I have no broken bones.' He stood up again, but with a cry of pain.

A little daylight remained, and the moon was brightening. I could see him clearly. He wore a riding coat with a fur collar. He had a dark face, with hard features, a heavy forehead and eyes which were angry just now. He was past youth, but had not yet reached middle age. I felt no fear of him. If he had been a good-looking young gentleman, if he had smiled and refused my offer cheerfully and with thanks, I would have gone on my way, but the roughness of the traveller relaxed me. So when he waved me to go, I remained where I was, saying:

'I cannot think of leaving you, sir, at such a late hour, in this lonely place, until I see that you are fit to get on your horse.'

He looked directly at me for the first time.

'I should think you ought to be at home yourself,' he said. 'Where do you come from?'

'From just below.'

'You live just below – do you mean at that house?' He pointed at Thornfield Hall.

'Yes, sir,'

'Whose house is it?'

'Mr Rochester's.'

'Do you know Mr Rochester?'

'No, I've never seen him.'

'You are not a servant at the Hall, of course. You are –' He stopped, looked at my simple dress, and seemed puzzled.

'I am the governess.'

'Ah, the governess!' he repeated. 'I had forgotten.' In two minutes he rose from the stile. His face expressed pain as he tried to move.

'You may help me a little,' he said, 'if you will be so kind. I must beg you to come here.'

I came. 'Excuse me,' he continued. 'I have to make use of you.' He laid a heavy hand on my shoulder and, leaning on me with some force, moved towards his horse. Having caught it, he controlled it immediately and jumped onto its back.

'Now,' he said, 'just hand me my whip. It is over by those bushes.'

I found it.

'Thank you. Now get home as fast as you can.'

A touch of his heel, and horse, dog and man had disappeared down the hill.

I walked on to the village with my letter, a little excited. It was a small event, but it marked with change one hour of my dull life.

◆

Jane falls in love with Mr Rochester, her employer, but Rochester shows no interest in Jane. He is older than she is, and he is an extremely wealthy man. Why would he be interested in a poor, plain governess like her? Besides, he is engaged to the beautiful Miss Ingram. But then, one night, he meets Jane in the garden.

Rochester declares his love for Jane

It was now the sweetest hour of the twenty-four. Sunset was giving way to moonrise. I found a path where I could wander unseen, but it was not long before something made me pause – not a sound, not a sight, but a smell. This new smell did not come from a leaf or flower. It was – I knew it well – Mr Rochester's tobacco. I saw him in the distance, and I stepped to one side to a sheltered seat. 'If I sit still,' I thought, 'he will never see me.'

He wandered around, examining the fruit on the bushes, and then bending towards a flowering plant. A great insect went noisily by me and settled near his foot. He saw it, and turned to look at it more closely.

'Now he has his back towards me,' I thought. 'Perhaps if I walk softly, I can move quietly away unnoticed.'

I walked gently across a grassy border, but as I crossed his shadow, thrown long over the garden by the moon, he said quietly, without turning round:

'Come back, Jane. On such a beautiful night it is a shame to remain indoors.'

It is one of my faults that, though my tongue is sometimes ready enough with an answer, there are times when it fails sadly in making an excuse; and this weakness always appears at some strange moment, when a simple word is needed to get out of a difficult situation. It failed me now.

'Jane,' he began again, as we walked, 'Thornfield is a pleasant place in summer, isn't it? Wouldn't you be sorry to leave it?'

'Must I leave, sir?'

'I am sorry, Jane, but I believe you must.'

'Then you *are* going to be married, sir?'

'In about a month I hope to bring back my bride. I have already, through her mother, heard of a place that I think will suit you. It is to educate the five daughters of a lady in the west of Ireland.'

'It is a long way away, sir.'

'Never mind. A girl of your sense will not complain about the journey or the distance. We have been good friends, Jane, haven't we?'

'Yes, sir.'

'I shall never see you again. I suppose that you will forget me?'

'That I *never* would, sir. You know . . .' It was impossible to continue.

'Jane, do you hear that bird singing in the wood?'

As I listened, I cried. I could hide my feelings no longer. When I did speak, it was to express a passionate wish that I had never been born, or ever come to Thornfield.

The violence of my feelings, excited by sadness and love, was gaining control, and demanding permission to win and speak.

'I love Thornfield – I love it because I have lived in it a full and happy life, for a short time at least. I have not been scorned or badly treated. I have talked, face to face, with what I enjoy – with a strong and original mind. I have known you, Mr Rochester, and I find it unbearable that I must be separated from you for ever. I see that I have to leave, and it is like having to die.'

'Why do you have to leave?'

'You, sir, have placed the need in front of me, in the form of your bride.'

'My bride! I have no bride!'

'But you will have.'

'Yes! I will! I will!'

'Then I tell you I must go!' I replied, moved to something like passion. 'Do you think I can stay to become nothing to you? Do you think I am a machine without feelings? Do you think that, because I am poor and plain, I am soulless and heartless? You think wrong! And if God had given me some beauty and great wealth, I would have made it as hard for you to leave me as it is for me to leave you. I am not talking to you now according to the usual custom. It is my spirit that talks to your spirit, before God, equals, as we are!'

'As we are!' repeated Mr Rochester. 'So,' he added, holding me in his arms. 'So, Jane!'

'Yes, so, sir,' I replied, 'but in fact not so; you are going to marry a person who is not good enough for you – one whom I do not believe that you truly love. I would scorn such a union; therefore I am better than you – let me go!'

'Where, Jane? To Ireland?'

'Yes, to Ireland. I have said what I think, and can go anywhere now.'

'Jane, be still; don't struggle, like a wild bird.'

'I am no bird. I am a free human being with an independent will, which I am now using to leave you.'

Another effort set me free.

'You *will* decide your own future,' he said. 'I offer you my hand, my heart, and a share of all my possessions.'

I was silent. I thought he was laughing at me.

'Do you doubt me, Jane?'

'Completely.'

'You do not trust me?'

'Not a bit.'

'Am I a liar in your eyes?' he asked passionately. 'Little doubter, I will make you believe me! What love have I for Miss Ingram? None. What love has she for me? I caused a story to reach her that my fortune was not a third of what was supposed, and when I visited her to see the result, it was coldness from her and her mother. I would not – I could not – marry Miss Ingram. I have only tried to make you jealous. I love you as much as I love myself. You – poor and plain as you are – I beg you to accept me as a husband!'

I began – as a result of his seriousness and especially his plain speaking – to believe his sincerity.

'Do you truly love me? Do you really wish me to be your wife?'

'I do. I promise you.'

'Then I will marry you.'

He pulled me to him. 'Make my happiness – I will make yours. God forgive me! Let no man prevent me: I have her and I will keep her.'

'There is no one to prevent us marrying, sir. I have no relations to make it their business.'

'No – that is the best of it,' he said. If I had loved him less, I would have thought his voice and look of victory wild. 'I know that my God approves of what I do. For the world's judgement, I care nothing.'

But what had happened to the night? The moon was clouded over, and wind was beginning to shake the trees. A flash lit up the sky, and there was a crack, a crash.

'We must go in,' said Mr Rochester. 'The weather is changing. It is a pity I could not sit with you here until morning, Jane.'

The rain poured down.

13   *A Tale of Two Cities*   Charles Dickens

Charles Dickens (1812–70) is one of the most famous writers in the world. His first novel, *The Pickwick Papers*, was published in monthly parts in 1836. He then wrote many other novels, including *Oliver Twist* (1837–39), *A Christmas Carol* (1843), *David Copperfield* (1849–50) and *Great Expectations* (1860–61). Dickens was a great observer of people and places, and had a deep understanding of human nature. Most of his novels describe characters and scenes that were typical of life in mid-nineteenth century London.

A Tale of Two Cities (1859), however, is set in Paris and London at the time of the French Revolution (1789–99). It is the story of Sydney Carton, a noble-minded but unambitious man, who falls in love with a French girl, Lucie Manette. She, however, falls in love with and marries Charles Darnay, a Frenchman who looks very similar to Carton. Darnay, a member of the once rich and powerful Evrémonde family, is captured by the revolutionary government and put in a Paris prison. Carton, out of love for Lucie, helps Darnay to escape and takes his place in the prison. He is ready to sacrifice everything for the happiness of the woman he loves, even his life. In this extract, Carton is waiting to be taken to the guillotine.

Sydney Carton goes to the guillotine

There were sounds, sounds whose meaning he understood: he was ready for them. Several doors were opened one after another, and then his own. A prison guard, with a list in his hand, looked in and said: 'Follow me, Evrémonde.' Sydney got up and followed him until he came to a large, dark room. It was half filled with people, brought there to have their arms tied. Some were standing; some were seated; some were crying, and a few were walking restlessly about. But most of them were silent and still, their eyes lowered.

Sydney stood by the wall in a dark corner. One man stopped as he passed, ready to greet him, but then went on. A few moments later, a young woman rose from the place where she had been sitting and came to speak to him. She had a slight girlish form, and a sweet thin face in which there was no sign of colour.

'Citizen Evrémonde,' she said, touching him with her cold hand, 'I am a poor little dressmaker who was with you in La Force.'

'True,' he replied. 'I forget what you were accused of?'

'Spying. But Heaven knows that I am not guilty. Who would think a poor, weak creature like me was a spy?'

She smiled so sadly as she spoke that tears came into Sydney's eyes.

'I am not afraid to die — I have done nothing wrong. If the Republic, which is going to do so much good to the poor, will profit from my death, I am ready to die. But how can my death be of use? Such a poor, weak creature!'

Great pity filled Sydney's heart as he looked at her and listened to her. She was the last person that he would ever speak to.

'I heard that you were freed, Citizen Evrémonde. I hoped it was true.'

'It was. But I was taken again.'

'If they let us ride together, Citizen Evrémonde, will you let me hold your hand? I am not afraid, but I am small and weak, and it will give me courage.'

As she lifted her patient eyes to his, he saw a sudden doubt in them, and then surprise. He pressed her work–worn, hunger–worn hands and touched them with his lips.

'Are you dying for him?' she whispered.

'Ssh! Yes. And for his wife and child.'

'Oh, will you let me hold your hand, brave stranger?'

'Ssh! Yes, my poor sister; to the last.' . . .

. . . The death-carts were passing slowly along the streets of Paris. Six carts carried the day's offering to the guillotine. As the wheels turned, they seemed to force their way through the people in the streets, but those who lived there were so used to the sight that there was nobody at all in many of the windows.

Of the riders in the carts, some looked around at their last roadside with calm, uninterested eyes; some were sunk, with their heads bent, in silent misery; some, remembering how they must seem to others, gave the crowds looks of pride.

There was a guard of horsemen riding at the side of the carts, and faces were often turned up to the horsemen as people in the street asked the names of the prisoners. On the steps of a church, waiting for the coming of the carts, stood Barsad the spy. He looked into the first cart. 'Not there.' He looked into the second. 'Not there.' His face cleared as he looked into the third.

'Which is Evrémonde?' said a man behind him.

'That one. At the back there.'

'With his hand in the girl's?'

'Yes.'

'Down with Evrémonde!' cried the man.

'Don't say that!' begged the spy nervously.

'And why not, citizen?'

'He is going to pay the price. It will be paid in five minutes more. Let him be at peace.'

But the man continued to shout, 'Down with Evrémonde!' The face of Evrémonde was turned towards him for a moment. Evrémonde saw the spy and the cart passed on.

The clocks struck three. In front of the guillotine, seated on chairs, were a number of women, busily knitting. The carts began to empty their loads and the guillotine began. Crash! A head was held up and the knitting women counted, 'One!' Crash! They counted, 'Two!'

The man they thought was Evrémonde got down from his cart, and the dressmaker was lifted out after him. He still held her patient hand and gently placed her with her back to the crashing engine that regularly rose and fell. She looked into his face and thanked him.

'Without you, dear stranger, I would not be so calm. I am naturally faint of heart, and a poor little thing. I think you are sent from Heaven to me.'

'Or you to me,' said Sydney Carton. 'Keep your eyes on me, dear child, and think of nothing else.'

'I mind nothing while I hold your hand. I shall mind nothing when I let it go, if they are quick.'

'They will be quick. Fear not!'

She kissed him; he kissed her; they prayed together. The little hand was not shaking as he let it go. In her face there was nothing worse than a sweet, bright patience. She went next, before him. The knitting-women counted, 'Twenty-two!'

The sound of many voices; the upturning of many faces; the noise of many footsteps in the crowd; all flashed away. 'Twenty-three!'

They said of him, in the city that night, that it was the most peaceful face ever seen there.

If Carton had spoken his own thoughts, they would have been these:

'I see Barsad, Cly, Defarge, and the judges – long rows of cruel men – dying by this guillotine before it stops its present work. I see a beautiful city rising in this terrible place, and I see that gradually this evil will die away.

'I see the lives for which I lay down my life, peaceful, useful and happy, in that England which I shall not see again. I see Lucie with a son on her breast, who bears my name. I see her father, old and bent, but well and at peace.

'I see Lucie, an old woman, crying for me as she remembers this day. I see her and her husband, when their lives are over, lying side by side in their last earthly bed, and I know that each was not more honoured in the other's soul than I was in the souls of both.

'I see that child who lay on her breast and who bore my name, now grown to be a man. He is making his way along that path of life that was once mine. I see him doing so well that my name is made famous there by the light of his. I see him, the fairest of judges and most respected of men, bringing a boy with golden hair to this place — and I hear him tell the child my story in a gentle voice.

'It is a far, far better thing that I do than I have ever done; it is a far, far better rest that I go to than I have ever known.'

14   *The Disappearance of Lady Frances Carfax*
from *Sherlock Holmes Short Stories*
Sir Arthur Conan Doyle

Sir Arthur Conan Doyle (1859-1930) created Sherlock Holmes, the world's most famous fictional detective. The first Holmes mystery, *A Study in Scarlet*, appeared in 1887. Conan Doyle wrote fifty-six short stories and four novels about Holmes and his friend and colleague, Dr Watson.

In this story, Lady Frances Carfax has disappeared. She was last seen in a hotel in Switzerland. Holmes is busy in London, so he sends Watson to Switzerland to speak to Marie Devine, Lady Frances's servant. In this extract, Holmes uses the energies and passion of wounded love to help him solve a mystery — although without informing Watson of his plans! Watson himself tells the story.

Dr Watson has an unpleasant experience

Next I went to Montpellier to see Marie Devine. She was very helpful. She had been fond of Lady Frances and completely loyal to her, she said, but recently Lady Frances had not been kind to her, and had even once accused her of stealing.

I asked her about the cheque for fifty pounds.

'It was a present, sir,' she replied. 'I am going to be married soon.'

We then spoke of the strange Englishman.

'Ah, he is a bad man, sir!' said Marie. 'A violent man. I myself have seen him seize Lady Frances by the wrist, and hurt her. It was by the lake at Lausanne, sir.'

Marie was sure that fear of this man was the cause of Lady Frances's sudden journeys. The poor lady was trying to escape from him.

'But look, sir!' Marie suddenly said. 'He's out there – the man himself!' She sounded frightened.

I looked out of the window. A very tall, dark man with a large black beard was walking slowly down the centre of the street, looking up at the numbers of the houses. It was clear that, like myself, he was looking for Marie. I ran out of the house and spoke to him angrily.

'You are an Englishman,' I said.

'I don't want to speak to you,' he said rudely.

'May I ask what your name is?'

'No, you may not!' he answered.

It was a difficult situation. The only way to deal with it was to use the direct method of shock.

'Where is Lady Frances Carfax?' I asked.

He looked at me in surprise.

'What have you done with her?' I continued. 'Why have you been following her? I want an answer from you immediately!'

The man gave a shout of anger and jumped on me. I am not a weak man, but he was as strong as a horse. He fought like a devil, and soon his hands were round my throat. I was nearly unconscious when a French workman rushed out of a small hotel and saved me. He struck the Englishman on the arm with his stick: this made him loosen his hold on my throat.

The wild man then stood near us for a moment, unable to decide whether to attack me again. Finally he turned angrily away and went into the house where Marie lived. I began to thank the kind Frenchman beside me.

'Well, Watson,' the 'Frenchman' said, 'you haven't done very well this time! I think you had better come back with me to London by the night train.'

An hour later Sherlock Holmes, wearing his own clothes now, was with me in my private sitting room at my hotel.

'I did not expect to be able to get away from London,' he said, 'but here I am after all!'

'And how did you know that I would be here in Montpellier?' I asked him.

'It was easy to guess that Montpellier would be the next stage of your travels,' Holmes said. 'Since I arrived I have been sitting in that small hotel, waiting for you. And really, Watson, what a situation you have got into!'

'Perhaps you would not have done better if you had been here yourself,' I answered, annoyed.

'I *have* done better, Watson!'

Just then one of the hotel servants brought somebody's card in. Holmes looked at it.

'Ah, here is Mr Philip Green. Mr Green is staying at this hotel, and he may be able to help us to find out what has happened to Lady Frances Carfax.'

The man who came in was the same violent person who had attacked me in the street. He did not look pleased when he saw me.

'I received your letter, Mr Holmes,' he said. 'But why is this man here? In what way can he be connected with the affair?'

'This is my old friend Dr Watson,' replied Holmes. 'He is helping us in this case.'

The stranger held out his large brown hand.

'I am very sorry about what happened, Dr Watson,' he said. 'When you blamed me for hurting Frances I lost control of myself. I am in a terrible state, you know. I don't understand this

57

affair at all. And, Mr Holmes, I don't even know who told you of my existence!'

'I have spoken to Miss Dobney, Lady Frances's old nurse,' Holmes said.

'Old Susan Dobney with the funny hat!' said Green. 'I remember her well.'

'And she remembers you. She knew you in the days before you went to South Africa.'

'Ah, I see that you know my whole story. I will not hide anything from you, Mr Holmes. I have loved Frances all my life. When I was a young man I made a few mistakes and got into trouble. And she was always so pure and good! So when somebody told her how I was living, she refused to speak to me again. But she certainly loved me. She loved me well enough to remain single. I stayed in South Africa for many years, and I became rich there. When I came back to Europe, I decided to find her – to try to persuade her to marry me. I found her in Lausanne, and I think I almost persuaded her, but her will was strong. The next time I went to her hotel I was told that she had left town. I followed her as far as Baden-Baden, and then after a time I learned that her servant was here. I am a rough sort of person; I have had a rough sort of life, and when Dr Watson spoke to me as he did I became quite wild for a moment. But, Mr Holmes, tell me what has happened to Lady Frances!'

'We will do our best to find that out,' said Holmes in a serious voice.

15   *Othello*
from *More Tales from Shakespeare*
Charles and Mary Lamb

William Shakespeare (1564–1616) was born in Stratford-upon-Avon, and by 1592 he was famous in London as an actor and writer. Over the next twenty years he wrote thirty-eight plays; most of these are considered to be masterpieces. He also wrote a lot of great poetry. Four hundred years later, he is still the most popular and famous writer in the English language.

In 1807 Charles Lamb and his sister, Mary Lamb, were asked to write the stories from the best known of Shakespeare's plays in a way that children could easily understand. Their adaptations of the stories were a great success.

Othello, first performed in 1604, is a tragedy about jealousy in love. The great achievement of the play is the description of the relationship between Othello, a Moor* who is a general in the Venetian army, and Iago, his trusted friend and adviser. When Iago tells Othello that his wife, Desdemona, is secretly in love with Cassio, another officer in the army, Othello believes him. The reasons for Iago's lies about Desdemona are never fully explained, but this only adds to the tragedy of the situation. In this extract the seeds of jealousy are growing in Othello's heart.

Othello suspects his wife

From that moment Othello was never happy. Nothing could ever bring back that sweet rest which he had enjoyed only yesterday. He grew tired of his job. He took no pleasure in his work. His heart, which used to jump with excitement at the sight of soldiers ready for battle or the sound of a drum, had lost all pride and purpose. His eagerness and all his old joys disappeared.

Sometimes he thought that his wife was honest, and at times he thought that she was not. Sometimes he thought that Iago was right, and at times he thought that he was wrong.

'I would have been happier if I'd never found out,' he thought.

If she loved Cassio, it made no difference to him, but he did not want to know. Torn to pieces by such thoughts as these, he

---

*Moor: a Muslim from north-west Africa

seized Iago's throat on one occasion and demanded proof of Desdemona's guilt; he threatened him with death for lying about her if there *was* no proof.

Pretending to be angry because his honesty was being doubted, Iago asked Othello if he had not sometimes seen a handkerchief spotted with berries in his wife's hand.

Othello answered that he had given it to her, and that it was his first gift.

'I saw Michael Cassio today with that same handkerchief,' said Iago.

'If you are telling the truth,' said Othello, 'I will not rest until my revenge has swallowed them up. First, to prove your loyalty, I expect Cassio to be put to death within three days. Then I will go away and think of a quick method of death for that beautiful devil, my wife.'

To a jealous man, small and unimportant things are strong proofs. A handkerchief of his wife's seen in Cassio's hand was reason enough for the deceived Othello to send them both to their death, without even asking how Cassio had obtained it. Desdemona had never given such a present to Cassio, and neither Cassio nor Desdemona were guilty of any offence against Othello. The evil Iago had made his wife (a good but weak woman) steal this handkerchief from Desdemona, pretending that she wanted to have a copy made. But Iago's real purpose was to leave it where Cassio would find it, and so give support to his suggestion that it was a present from Desdemona.

Meeting his wife soon afterwards, Othello pretended that he had a headache, and asked her to lend him her handkerchief to hold to his head and reduce the pain.

She did so.

'Not this,' said Othello, 'but that handkerchief I gave you.'

Desdemona had not got it with her (because it had been stolen, as we have said).

'What have you done?' said Othello. 'An Egyptian woman gave that handkerchief to my mother. She told her that while she kept it, my father would love her. If she lost it, or gave it away, my father's love would change and he would hate her as much as he had loved her. When she was dying, she gave it to me. She told me to give it to my wife if I ever married.'

'Is it possible?' said the frightened lady.

'It is true,' continued Othello, 'it is a magic handkerchief.'

Desdemona was ready to die with fear. She knew that she had lost it, and she feared that with it she had lost her husband's love.

Othello continued to demand the handkerchief. When she could not produce it, she tried to turn her husband away from such serious thoughts. She cheerfully suggested that all his talk about the handkerchief was meant to prevent her from speaking for Michael Cassio, whom she began to praise (as Iago had said she would). Othello hurried out of the room in anger, and then Desdemona began to suspect that her lord was jealous.

She could not think what cause she had given him for this, so then she blamed herself for thinking so badly of the noble Othello. She thought that perhaps some unpleasant news from Venice or some state troubles had made him angry.

'Men are not gods,' she told herself. 'We must not expect such gentleness from them when they are married as they show us on the wedding day.' Then she was angry with herself again for judging his unkindness so unkindly.

When Othello and Desdemona met again, he accused her more clearly of being unfaithful, and of loving another man whom he did not name. He told her that he was ready to suffer all sorts of evils bravely — illness, shame, lack of money — but her unfaithfulness had broken his heart. While he swore at her, he also said that she looked so beautiful and smelt so sweet.

'Why was I ever born?' he cried . . .

. . . When he had left her, this poor lady was so filled with confusion at her lord's false accusations that she felt ready to fall into a deep sleep and told her servant to prepare her bed. When people teach their babies, she thought, they do it gently.

'Why couldn't Othello be gentle like that?' she wondered. This was her only complaint.

Desdemona went to bed expecting her lord to follow her. As soon as she had fallen into a troubled sleep, though, Othello entered the room intending to put his lady to death. When he saw her asleep, he thought he would not make her bleed or mark that beautiful white skin of hers. But he had decided that she should die. If not (as he said), she would live to be unfaithful to more men, as she had been to him. Then he kissed her for the last time, but that kiss was so sweet that he was forced to kiss her again.

Desdemona was woken by his kisses. She looked at Othello, saw him bite his bottom lip and roll his eyes, and knew that he was dangerous when he looked like this. He told her to prepare for death, and to say her prayers, because he would not kill her soul.

This guiltless wife begged for pity, and asked to know her crime. Then he named Cassio, and the handkerchief which (he said) she had given him. Desdemona began to explain, but Othello suddenly refused to hear any more. He covered her face with the bedclothes, and stopped her breathing until she died.

16 *The Warden* Anthony Trollope

Anthony Trollope (1815–82) had a successful career in the Post Office. (He designed the red post box, which is still familiar in English streets.) He is, of course, more famous as a writer. His descriptions of provincial middle class life were very popular with the reading public. His best work shows a sensitive and detailed understanding of human nature.

The Warden (1855) is a study of the clash between public duty and individual conscience. The Reverend Septimus Harding, the warden of a small old people's home, is a gentle man, without much understanding of the outside world. He never thinks about the big difference between his comfortable salary and the small amount of money given to the old men in his home. John Bold, a young local reformer, thinks that the men in the home should receive more money from Mr Harding. The local newspaper becomes interested, and accuses Mr Harding of being greedy and dishonest. In this extract, Eleanor Harding, the warden's daughter, visits John Bold, who is in love with her.

Eleanor Harding and John Bold

As Eleanor lay awake in bed that night, she formed a plan. She would go personally to John Bold and beg him to drop the legal action which he had begun. She would do this for her father. Of course she could not offer herself as a reward – that would be quite improper. Though she might continue secretly to love John Bold, any question of marriage was naturally at an end.

Finally she slept and she rose full of hope the following morning. She knew that John Bold was in London but was expected home soon, so she went to visit Mary, to arrange with her a plan for a meeting with her brother. However, on entering the Bolds' sitting room, she was surprised to see John's stick and coat and various bags, which showed that he had returned.

'John came back very suddenly,' said Mary. 'He has been travelling all night.'

'Then I'll come again some other time,' said Eleanor, in some confusion.

'He will be out for the next two hours,' said Mary. 'He's with that horrible Mr Finney. He came only to see him and he goes back again to London on the night train.'

Eleanor, who had not intended to have her interview with Bold that day, realized that such a meeting must be held now or never.

'Mary,' she began, 'I must see John before he goes back.'

'Of course,' said Mary, secretly rather surprised. 'I know he'll be delighted to see you.'

'I must see him now, today, and beg him to do me a special service,' went on Eleanor with great seriousness. 'But when I have done so, there can never be anything more between us.' And she began to explain her plan for saving her father.

It was clear that Mary Bold did not follow her line of thought. It seemed quite natural that Eleanor should try to speak to Bold's better feelings with reference to her father, and it seemed to Mary quite natural that John should give way, affected by such sincere tears and pretty looks. But why his good nature should not be rewarded, when the reward would help everyone and hurt no one, was a point which her practical nature could not understand, and she said so.

'But I am sure you love him, don't you?' argued Mary. 'And I am sure he loves you better than anything in the world.'

Eleanor tried to answer, but her eyes filled with tears, so she walked to the window, pretending to blow her nose, and when she recovered herself she said as firmly as she could, 'Mary, this is nonsense.'

'But you do love him,' Mary said. 'You love him with all your heart. You cannot deny it.'

'I . . .' began Eleanor, and finally burst into tears, admitting to Mary that she did love John but that it would make no difference to her decision.

While they were still talking, Bold returned and Eleanor was forced to take action. She decided to carry out her original plan and ran into her friend's bedroom to wash the tears from her face.

'Tell him that I am here,' she said to Mary, 'and that I shall join you both soon. And remember, whatever you do, don't leave us alone together.' Eleanor then washed her face with extreme care, thinking always of her poor father; but she also managed to improve the arrangement of a curl or two and give some added colour to her lips, to be sure that she would make a good impression.

John Bold had not seen her since the day they had met walking near the cathedral, but during this time he had often thought of her and considered a hundred ways of showing her how pure his love was. Sometimes when he woke in the morning he even felt like putting a gun to his head, but this was usually after a late-night party with Tom Towers, his friend who was a reporter for the *Jupiter*.

How beautiful Eleanor seemed to him as she walked slowly into the room. The care she had taken with her appearance was now having its effect. She had never looked lovelier to her admirer than she did now. Her face was serious but full of movement, and her full, dark eyes shone with nervous energy.

He began to talk – about London, about Barchester, about the weather – and then asked about Mr Harding's health.

'My father is not very well,' said Eleanor. 'I especially want to speak to you about my father, Mr Bold. He is very unhappy about this business of the hospital. You would pity him, Mr Bold, if you could see the suffering it has caused him.'

'Oh, Miss Harding!'

'He is a changed man. And if this goes on, he will die; he will break his heart and die. I am sure it was not you, Mr Bold, who wrote those cruel things in the newspaper.'

'It was not,' cried John Bold, who was beginning to feel extremely guilty about his friendship with Tom Towers.

'No, I'm sure it was not; you would not be so cruel. But they have called my father greedy and dishonest, and they say that he is robbing the old men and taking the money of the hospital for nothing.'

'I have never said so, Miss Harding. I . . .'

'No,' continued Eleanor, interrupting him, the tide of her feelings carrying her on. 'No, I am sure you have not, but others have said so. And if such things are said or written again, they will kill him! You know, I'm sure, that he is not interested in money.'

Brother and sister were both quick to agree on this point.

'It is kind of you to say so, Mary, and of you too, Mr Bold. He would leave the hospital tomorrow, and give up his house and the income and everything, if the archdeacon . . .' Here she almost said 'would allow it' but instead added, 'Oh, why did all this have to happen?'

'No one who knows Mr Harding personally can possibly accuse him of doing wrong,' said Bold.

'But he is the one whom you are punishing. He is the one who is suffering,' said Eleanor. 'He has never had an unkind thought in his life, never spoken an unkind word.' At this moment she burst into tears so violent that she could not speak.

For the fifth or sixth time Bold tried to say that neither he nor his friends blamed Mr Harding personally.

'Then why are you punishing him?' cried Eleanor through her tears. 'Why are you wrecking his life? Oh, Mr Bold, why did you begin all this? You whom we all so − so − valued!'

John Bold tried his best to excuse himself, with references to his public duty, and repeated how highly he valued Mr Harding's character.

By now Eleanor was again in control of herself. 'Mr Bold,' she said, 'I have come here to beg you to give up this action.'

He stood up from his seat and looked extremely unhappy and uncomfortable.

'I beg you to give it up, I beg you to spare my father, to spare his life and his health, before one or the other is destroyed. I know how much I am asking and how little right I have to ask anything, but it is not for myself − it is for my father. Oh, Mr Bold, I beg you, do this for us; do not drive to desperation a man who has loved you so well.'

She did not actually kneel in front of him, but she let her soft hands rest pitifully on his arm. What pleasure this would have given him if the circumstances had been different! But what could he say to her now? How could he explain that the matter was probably beyond his control, that he could not now silence the storm which he had created?

'Surely, John, you cannot refuse her,' said his sister.

'I would give my life itself,' he said, 'if it would be of use to her.'

'Oh, Mr Bold, do not say that. I ask nothing for myself. I'm only asking for my father something that is in your power to give.'

'I would give her anything,' said Mr Bold wildly, still talking to his sister. 'Everything I have is hers if she will accept it: my house, my heart. Every hope I have is fixed on her. Her smiles are sweeter to me than the sun, and when I see her sad as she is now, every nerve in my body aches. No man can love her better than I love her.'

'No, no, no,' cried Eleanor, 'there can be no talk of love between us. Will you protect my father from the evil which you have brought on him?'

'Oh, Eleanor, I will do anything. Let me tell you how I love you.'

'No, no, no,' she almost screamed. 'This is improper of you, Mr Bold. Will you leave my father to die in peace, quietly in his quiet home? I will not leave you till you promise me.' She held on to his arm as she followed him across the room. 'Promise me, promise me,' she cried. 'Say that my father is safe. One word will do. I know how honest you are; say one word and I will let you go.' Still she held him, looking eagerly into his face. Her hair was loose, her eyes were red but he thought he had never seen her look so lovely. 'Promise me,' she said. 'I will not leave you till you promise me.'

'I will,' he said at last. 'All I can do, I will do.'

'Then may God protect you!' said Eleanor, and began to cry like a child. Exhausted, she wanted to go now, but Bold wished to explain the situation concerning her father, and she felt the need to stay and listen to him.

Bold explained that the action against the hospital was something which he alone had started; but that now many other people had become interested in the matter, some of whom were much more powerful than himself. However, the lawyers turned to him for their instructions and, more importantly, for the payment of their bills, and he promised that he would tell them at once that he wished to give up the case. He then suggested that he would ride over to see Dr Grantly that same afternoon, to tell him of the change in his intentions, and for this reason he would delay his immediate return to London.

All of this was very pleasant to hear, and Eleanor began to enjoy the satisfaction of feeling that she had succeeded in her purpose. She now got up to fetch her hat.

'Are you going so soon?' said Bold. 'May I not say one word for myself?'

'*I'll* fetch your hat, Eleanor,' said Mary, leaving the room.

'Mary, Mary, don't go!' cried Eleanor, but it was too late.

Now they were alone, John Bold poured out the feelings of his heart and this time Eleanor's 'no, no, no,' had no effect. She was pressed to say whether her father would be against their marriage; whether she found him acceptable; whether she preferred someone else; whether she could possibly love him; and other similar things. To each of these questions she was forced to give replies, so when she finally left the Bolds' home she felt that she had succeeded very well in part of her intention (to save her father) but had completely failed in the other part (to refuse any further contact with John).

Eleanor returned home not unhappy but not completely satisfied with herself. She felt annoyed with Mary, who had shown herself to be less dependable than expected. All she could do now, she thought, was to inform her father that John Bold was her accepted lover.

17   *The Prisoner of Zenda*   Anthony Hope

Anthony Hope (1863–1933) was a lawyer until 1894, when *The Prisoner of Zenda* was published. It was a great success and won praise from many other writers, including Robert Louis Stevenson. One of the main characters appeared in a second novel, *Rupert of Hentzau* (1898), which was equally popular.

The Prisoner of Zenda is about two men who look very similar to each other. Rudolf Rassendyll, an English adventurer and the narrator of the story, changes places with the King of Ruritania, and falls in love with the beautiful Princess Flavia, the King's future bride. The Princess loves Rudolf, without realizing that he is not the real King. In this extract, Rudolf sees Princess Flavia soon after she has discovered the truth.

Rudolf declares his love for Princess Flavia

Outside, Fritz did not turn the way we had come, but went another way.

'Where are we going?' I asked.

'She has sent for you. When it is over, come back to the bridge. I'll wait there.'

'What does she want?' I asked breathlessly. He shook his head. 'Does she know everything?'

'Yes, everything.'

He opened a door, gently pushed me in, and left me. It was a room filled with beautiful furniture, and in the middle of it stood the Princess. I walked up to her and fell on one knee and kissed her hand. Then, before I knew what I was saying, the word came out: 'Flavia!'

She shook a little as I rose to my feet and faced her.

'Don't stand, don't stand!' she cried. 'You mustn't! You're hurt. Sit down here – on this chair.'

She gently made me sit, and put her hand on my forehead.

'How hot your head is!' she said.

I had come to beg her forgiveness, but somehow love gives to even a dull man the knowledge of his lover's heart. So all I said was: 'I love you with all my heart and soul!'

What troubled and shamed her? Not her love for me, but the fear that I had pretended to love her as I had pretended to be the King.

'I love you,' I repeated. 'There will never be another woman in the world for me. But God forgive me the wrong I've done!'

'They made you do it,' she said quickly. 'It would have made no difference if I'd known. It was always you that I loved, never the King.'

'I tried to tell you – you remember when Sapt interrupted us on the night of the dance at Strelsau?'

'I know,' she answered softly. 'They have told me all.'

'I am going away tonight,' I said.

'No, no, no! Not tonight!'

'I must, before more people have seen me. And how could I stay . . .?'

'If I could come with you!' she whispered.

'Don't,' I cried, almost roughly, and moved away from her.

'You are right, Rudolf, dear,' she said. 'If love were all, I would follow you to the world's end. But is love the only thing? If you had believed that, you would have left the King to die in his prison.'

'I nearly did it, Flavia,' I whispered.

'But honour did not let you. Women too must behave

honourably, Rudolf. My honour lies in being loyal to my country. I shall always wear your ring.'

'And I yours,' I answered. Then I said goodbye and left her. I heard her saying my name over and over again . . .

18   *Sons and Lovers*   D. H. Lawrence

David Herbert Lawrence (1885-1930) is famous for his novels, short stories and poems. His novels were strongly criticized at the time for their sexual openness. His most well-known books include *The White Peacock* (1911), *The Rainbow* (1915), *Women in Love* (1920) and *Lady Chatterley's Lover* (1928), which did not appear in its complete form in England until 1960.

Sons and Lovers (1913) has always been one of Lawrence's most popular books, and the story is based on his own childhood. It describes Paul Morell's relationship with two very different women – the spiritual Miriam, and the more physical Clara Dawes – and his inability to find happiness with either of them because of his love for his mother. In this extract, Paul tries to find happiness with Miriam. But the shadow of his disapproving mother is never far away.

Paul and Miriam

That summer the cherry trees at the farm were heavy with fruit. They stood very tall, hung thick with bright red and dark red cherries. Paul and Edgar were gathering the fruit one evening. It had been a hot day and now the clouds were rolling in the sky, dark and warm. The wind made the whole tree swing with a movement that excited Paul. He sat unsteadily among the higher branches, feeling slightly drunk with the tree's movement, and tore off handful after handful of the smooth, cool fruit. Cherries touched his ears and neck as he leaned forward. Red-coloured fruit shone under the darkness of the leaves. The sun, going down, caught the broken clouds. Enormous piles of gold shone out in the south-east. The world, until now grey, was covered in golden light, making trees and grass and far-off water shine.

Miriam came out to watch.

'Oh,' Paul heard her call, 'isn't it wonderful!' He looked down. There was a pale light on the soft face turned up to him.

'How high you are!' she said.

He threw a handful of cherries at her. She was taken by surprise and was afraid. He laughed and rained more cherries down on her. She ran off to escape them, picking up some cherries on the way. She hung two fine pairs over her ears, then looked up again.

'Haven't you got enough?' she asked.

'Nearly. It's like being on a ship up here.'

'How long will you stay?'

'Till the sunset ends.'

She watched the golden clouds turn to orange, then rose, then reddish purple, until the passion went out of the sky. Paul climbed down with his basket.

'They're lovely,' said Miriam, feeling the cherries.

'I've torn my sleeve,' said Paul. It was near the shoulder. She put her fingers through the tear.

'How warm,' she said.

He laughed. There was a strange, new sound in his voice.

'Shall we walk a little way?' he said.

They went down the fields as far as a thick wood.

'Shall we go in among the trees?' he asked.

'Do you want to?'

'Yes.'

It was very dark in the wood. She was afraid. Paul was silent and strange. He seemed hardly conscious of her as a person: to him she was only a woman. He stood against a tree and took her in his arms. She gave herself to him, but feeling some sort of horror. This thick-voiced man was a stranger to her.

Later it began to rain. Paul lay with his head on the ground listening to the sharp sound of the raindrops. His heart was heavy. He realized that she had not been with him, that her soul had stood back. His body felt calmer but that was all. She put her hands over him to feel if he was getting wet.

'We must go,' said Miriam.

'Yes,' said Paul but did not move.

'The rain is coming in on us,' said Miriam.

He rose and helped her up. They walked hand in hand. A short time later, they went indoors. . . .

. . . They made love a number of times after this. Afterwards Paul always had the feeling of failure and death.

'You don't really want me when I come to you,' said Paul sadly after a week or two.

'No, don't say so,' she said, taking his head in her arms. 'Don't I want your children?'

'Shall we get married then?' said Paul.

'We're too young,' she said, after a pause. 'Not yet.'

With Paul the sense of failure grew stronger. At first it was only a sadness. Then he began to feel that he could not go on. He wanted to run, go abroad, anything. Gradually he stopped asking her to have him. He realized consciously that it was no good.

He told his mother that he would stop seeing Miriam. On Sunday he went up to the farm in the early afternoon. Miriam met him at the end of the farm road. She was wearing a new dress with short sleeves. She had made herself look so beautiful and fresh for him. They sat down. He lay with his head on her breast while she touched his hair. She knew that he was somehow 'absent'.

'I've been thinking,' he said finally, 'we ought to stop seeing each other.'

'What?' she cried in surprise.

'Because it's no good going on. I want us to finish – you to be free of me, I free of you.'

'How many times have you offered to marry me and I wasn't willing?'

'I know – but I want us to finish.'

'You're a child of four!' she said in her anger. 'And what can I tell my mother?' she asked.

'I told my mother that we would stop seeing each other,' he said.

'I shan't tell them at home,' she said. 'It's always been the same: one long battle between us – you fighting me off!'

'Not always – not at first,' he argued.

'Always – from the very beginning – always the same.'

He sat in silence. His heart was hard against her. He left her at the road-end. As she went home alone, in her new dress, having to face her family at the other end, he stood without moving on the high road, filled with pain and shame.

19　*Romeo and Juliet*
from *More Tales from Shakespeare*
Charles and Mary Lamb

William Shakespeare (1564–1616) was born in Stratford-upon-Avon, and by 1592 he was famous in London as an actor and writer. Over the next twenty years he wrote thirty-eight plays; most of these are considered to be masterpieces. He also wrote a lot of great poetry. Four hundred years later, he is still the most popular and famous writer in the English language.

In 1807 Charles Lamb and his sister, Mary Lamb, were asked to write the stories from the best known of Shakespeare's plays in a way that children could easily understand. Their adaptations of the stories were a great success.

Romeo and Juliet (1595) is one of Shakespeare's most famous tragedies. Set in Verona, it is the story of two young lovers, Romeo Montague and Juliet Capulet, who have to marry in secret because their families hate each other. Friar Lawrence, a friendly priest, agrees to marry them, hoping that this will stop the war between the two families. But their secret marriage is immediately followed by disaster. Romeo kills Juliet's cousin, Tybalt, in a fight and has to leave Verona for Mantua. Juliet's father, who does not know of his daughter's marriage to Romeo, arranges for her to marry Count Paris. On the day before Juliet is supposed to marry Paris, Friar Lawrence gives her some special medicine which will make her sleep for forty-two hours. Her family will think that she is dead, and will take her to the family grave. Then, when she wakes up, Romeo will arrive and take her away with him. In this extract, Romeo hears the news that Juliet is dead before Friar Lawrence's messenger can reach him to tell him the truth.

The death of Romeo and Juliet

When Romeo learnt that his wife was dead and could not be brought back to life with any kisses, he ordered horses to be got ready so that he could visit Verona that night and see his lady in her grave.

As evil is quick to enter into the thoughts of hopeless men, he remembered a poor medicine-seller in Mantua whom he had recently passed. He went to this man and told him that he wanted to buy some poison. The poor man put his doubts to one side when Romeo offered him some gold, and sold him a poison which, he said, would kill him quickly if he swallowed it.

With this poison Romeo set out for Verona to see his dear lady in her grave, intending then to take the poison and be buried by her side. He reached Verona at midnight and found the churchyard, in the middle of which stood the ancient grave of the Capulets. He had brought a light and some tools with him, and was just beginning to break open the door, when he was interrupted by a voice which called him by the name of 'evil Montague' and ordered him to stop his unlawful business.

It was Paris, who had come to the churchyard at this strange time of night to put flowers on Juliet's grave. He did not know why Romeo was there, but he knew that he was a Montague, an enemy of the Capulets; he thought, therefore, that he had come to do terrible things to the dead body. He angrily ordered him to stop, and called him a criminal who, by the laws of Verona, had to die.

Romeo begged Paris to leave him, and warned him not to make him angry. He reminded Paris of the death of Tybalt, who was also buried there. But Paris would not listen to his warning and tried to take him as a criminal. Then they fought, and Romeo killed him.

When Romeo saw who he had killed, he took the dead youth by the hand and said that he would bury him in Juliet's grave. He opened the grave, and there lay his lady, in perfect beauty, looking like one whom death had no power to change. She was as fresh as when she had fallen asleep; and near her lay Tybalt. When Romeo saw him, he begged forgiveness of his lifeless body, and, for Juliet, he called him 'cousin' and said that his enemy would soon be dead, too.

Now Romeo said his last goodbye to his lady, kissing her lips. Then he swallowed the poison which the medicine-seller had sold him. Its action was deadly and real, unlike the liquid which Juliet had drunk. The effect of her drug was now nearly at an end. . . .

. . . Friar Lawrence had by now learnt that the letters which he had sent to Mantua had, by some unlucky chance, never reached Romeo. So he came himself, with tools and a light, to free the lady from her early grave. But he was surprised to find a light already burning in the Capulets' grave, and to see swords and blood near it, and Romeo and Paris lying lifeless there.

Before he could imagine how these things had happened, Juliet woke out of her long sleep. Seeing the friar near her, she remembered where she was, and why she was there, and asked for Romeo.

Hearing a noise, the friar begged her to come out of that place of death and unnatural sleep, because a greater power than theirs had ruined all their plans. Then, frightened by the noise, he ran away.

When Juliet saw the cup in her true love's hand, she guessed that poison had been the cause of his death. She would have swallowed the same poison if Romeo had not drunk it all. She kissed his lips to see if poison was still on them. Then, hearing a noise of people coming nearer, she quickly pulled out a knife which Romeo wore, struck herself with it, and died by his side.

Extract Wordlist

ado	worry, or trouble
astonish	to surprise someone very much
archdeacon	an important person in the Church of England
avenue	a narrow road or path between two lines of trees
bride	a woman on her wedding day
candle	a wax stick with a piece of string through it that gives light when it burns
carriage	a passenger vehicle with wheels, pulled by a horse
cart	a vehicle pulled by a horse, used for carrying heavy things
cherry	a small, soft, round, red fruit with a stone in the middle
comrade	someone who fights on your side, in war or politics
confess	to admit
cottage	a small house in the country
courtship	the period of a romantic relationship before marriage
creep	to move very quietly
degrade	to reduce someone to a lower status or quality
divorce	a legal end to a marriage
engaged	your state after you have agreed to marry
fairy	a small, imaginary creature with magical powers
faithful	loyal, especially sexually
fancy dress	party clothes that make you look like someone else
friar	a religious man who teaches about religion
governess	a woman who lives with a rich family and teaches their children at home
guillotine	a piece of equipment used for cutting off people's heads during the French Revolution
hound	a dog used for hunting
inferior	of lower quality or status

knit	to make clothes from wool using two needles
misery	great unhappiness
murmur	a soft, continuous sound; to speak very quietly
noble	of excellent character and high principles
obscure	not clearly understood
passion	very strong, deeply felt emotion
prejudice	a dislike of someone for no good reason
relief	the feeling when something terrible ends
republic	a country with a president, not a king or queen
Reverend	a title of respect for a Christian minister
revolution	a time of sudden, often violent, political change
scorn	a feeling of no respect for someone or something
shrew	an unpleasant woman who argues a lot
spell	words used to perform magic on someone
stile	steps that help you climb over a fence
tale	a fictional story
tame	to train a wild animal to obey you
theology	the study of religion
warden	a person officially in charge of a church building
wicked	very bad; evil
will	a strong desire or wish to do something

ACTIVITIES

Pages 1–14

Before you read

1 Think about your perfect partner. Put these qualities in order of importance, and add one more quality. Then compare your list with another student's.

   faithfulness   intelligence   kindness   physical attractiveness   sense of humour

2 Look at the Extract Wordlist on pages 78–79. These words are all in the stories. Discuss which words are connected with love and/or marriage.

3 Find the words in *italics* in your dictionary. They are all used to introduce the stories.

   a Use these words in the phrases below.

   approve   basic   capitalist   classic   narrate   provincial   survive

   to ..... an accident   a ..... economy
   to ..... of a friend's boyfriend   a ..... salary
   to ..... a story   a ..... life
   a ..... film

   b Make three sentences with these words.

   – *adaptation, extract, masterpiece*
   – *household, housekeeper*
   – *companion, landlady*

After you read

4 In *Rebecca*, why does Mrs de Winter feel

   a worried?
   b surprised?
   c excited?
   d upset?

5 In *A Midsummer Night's Dream*, what is the relationship between
   a Helena and Demetrius?
   b Oberon and Puck?
   c Lysander and Hermia?
   d Hermia and Demetrius?

6 Act out this imaginary conversation between Susan Bell and Aaron Dunn from *The Courtship of Susan Bell*.
   Student A: You are Aaron. You are alone with Susan. Give her the drawing, and persuade her to keep it.
   Student B: You are Susan. You want to keep the drawing, but you feel that you cannot. Tell Aaron why.

7 In *Round the World in Eighty Days*, who do these words describe, and why?
   a worried
   b guilty
   c calm
   d happy

Pages 14–27

Before you read

8 The person you love is poor, already married, or rude and bad-tempered. Discuss which of these is the biggest problem, and why.

9 Are the sentences below true or false? Find the words in *italics* in your dictionary.
   a A *comedy* tries to make you cry.
   b An *estate* is a small piece of land.
   c If you *overcome* a problem, you find a solution.
   d Books are *published* before they are written.
   e *Revolutions* are often violent.
   f You always know how an *unstable* person will behave.

After you read

10 Which of these sentences about *Wuthering Heights* are false?
   a Cathy loves Heathcliff because he is good-looking.
   b Cathy tells Heathcliff that she loves him.

   c Nelly Dean approves of Cathy's marriage to Edgar.

   d Heathcliff and Cathy accuse each other of being cruel.

11 In *The Taming of the Shrew*, which of these sentences describes Petruchio's behaviour? Why does he behave like that?

   a He is rude and bad-tempered towards everybody.

   b He makes fun of Katharine in front of the servants.

   c He speaks gently to Katharine but shouts at the servants.

   d He threatens not to feed Katharine until she apologizes.

12 Work with another student. Act out this imaginary conversation from *Dr Zhivago*.

   Student A: You are Zhivago. Explain to Lara why you cannot see her again.

   Student B: You are Lara. Persuade Zhivago to continue seeing you.

Pages 27–44

Before you read

13 Which of these people is different from the others? Why?

Jane Austen   Sherlock Holmes   Thomas Hardy
William Shakespeare

14 Find these words in your dictionary. Which words can describe a character in a story?

conscience   declare   formidable   secondary   status   superior

After you read

15 Discuss whether, in *Pride and Prejudice*, these words describe Elizabeth's reaction to Darcy, Lady Catherine, or both?

polite   embarrassed   insulted   upset   scornful

16 In *The Hound of the Baskervilles*, how does Laura Lyons feel about Stapleton before Holmes's visit and after it? Why does she change her opinion of him?

17 Who says these lines in *Jude the Obscure*? What do the words in *italics* mean?

   a 'I wonder why we did *that*?'

   b '*It's* a lesson I ought to learn at this Easter season.'

   c '*That's* silly!'

d 'How has *that* happened?'

e '*That*'s why *he* didn't come today.'

18 Work with another student. Discuss what might happen in the next conversation between Benedick and Beatrice in *Much Ado About Nothing*. Then act out the conversation.

Pages 44–62

Before you read

19 Find the word *sacrifice* in your dictionary. Talk about a sacrifice that you have made. Why did you make it?

After you read

20 How are these important in *Jane Eyre*?

a ice

b Thornfield Hall

c a bird

d Miss Ingram

21 In *A Tale of Two Cities*, how does Sydney feel just before he dies? Why?

22 In *The Disappearance of Lady Frances Carfax*, why doesn't Lady Carfax want to marry Philip Green, do you think?

23 In *Othello*, who do the following words describe, and why?

a dishonest and evil

b confused and jealous

c innocent and afraid

Pages 62–77

Before you read

24 Find these words in your dictionary.

clash   Count   reformer

Which of them is

a a member of the upper classes in some countries

b a big disagreement or fight

c a person who wants political or social change

After you read

25 In *The Warden*, what is Eleanor Harding's original plan, and how successful is she?

26 Discuss how Princess Flavia, in *The Prisoner of Zenda*, feels when Rudolf says he loves her. Why?

27 Discuss words that describe the characters and feelings of Paul and Miriam in *Sons and Lovers*.

28 Finish these sentences about *Romeo and Juliet*.

    a If the friar's messenger had reached Mantua earlier, . . .

    b If Count Paris hadn't come to the churchyard, . . .

    c If Romeo hadn't drunk the poison, . . .

Writing

29 Choose one of the extracts you have read. Write the next part of the story from your imagination or – if you have read the whole book – from memory.

30 You are a character in one of the extracts. Describe your experience in a letter to a friend.

31 You are a journalist. Which character from one of the stories would you most like to interview? Write the interview for your newspaper. Say why you chose this particular character.

32 Imagine that you have fallen in love with a character from one of the stories. Write him/her a love letter. Say why they would be happier with you than with another character from their story.

33 Imagine you are making a film of one of these stories. Which famous actors would you choose to play the characters in your film, and why?

34 Write about the importance of one of these in the extracts you have read: gifts, money, goodbyes, fear or happiness.

BESTSELLING
PENGUIN READERS

AT LEVEL 5

The Body

The Firm

Four Weddings and a Funeral

The Great Gatsby

Jane Eyre

The Pelican Brief

The Prisoner of Zenda

Rebecca

Tales from Shakespeare

Taste and Other Tales

A Time to Kill

Wuthering Heights

THE BEST WEBSITES FOR STUDENTS OF ENGLISH!

www.penguinreaders.com

Where the world of Penguin Readers comes to life

- Fully searchable on-line catalogue
- Downloadable resource materials
- First ever on-line Penguin Reader!
- New competition each month!

www.penguindossiers.com

Up-to-the-minute website providing articles for free!

- Articles about your favourite stars, blockbuster movies and big sports events!
- Written in simple English with fun activities!

NEW from Penguin Readers
Your favourite titles on Audio CD

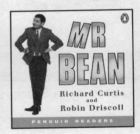

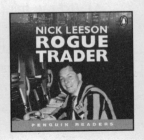